Reg Clay

This screenplay has been reformatted for print.

Copyright © 2018 Reg Clay

All rights reserved. No part of this book may be reproduced or transmitted in any form or by any means, electronic or mechanical, including photocopying, recording or by any information storage and retrieval system, without permission in writing from the publisher.

Independently Published– New Book Authors Madison, WI
ISBN 978-1-7915097-2-9
Four Men in Paris| Reg Clay

Available Formats: eBook | Paperback distribution

FOUR MEN IN PARIS first premiered at the Douglas Morrison Theatre (www.dmtonline.org), in Hayward, California on Friday, October 12th, 2018 – produced by Plethos Productions (www.plethos.org) – with the following cast:

RICHARD WRIGHT	....	Barry Graves
JAMES BALDWIN	....	Curtis Manning
CHESTER HIMES	....	S. Angelo Acevedo
OLLIE HARRINGTON	....	Peter Fitzsimmons
ELLEN WRIGHT	....	Kim Donovan
JULIA WRIGHT / FATIMA	....	Helaina Alvarez
VELVET	....	Priya Guyadeen
FRANCOIS	....	Joshua Flores
JEAN SARTRE / OFFICER	....	Michael Dorado
MARIGOLD	....	Laura Michler
DR. KING	....	Reg Clay

ACT ONE, Scene 1. Early morning. There is a beautiful half lit sunrise on the scrim; there are some images on stage, but it's mostly darkened. Ollie is center stage, well lit.

OLLIE

A beautiful, crisp, bright morning. The wind's a bit chilly, but nothing a brother who's seen an eternity of hard times can't handle. Beautiful mornings like this don't mean a damn thing to the ordinary black man – it's just another day of oppression and sadness. A morning that promises great things but at sundown, same ol crap. But this is Paris – this morning that shines on us black men is a good day. A day where we can stretch out our legs and our hearts and our minds. For here, we are free.

[CHESTER appears, from the café, walking and sitting at the table, sitting his coffee down with a manuscript under his arm]

CHESTER

Man, I got something good. Something good, this time.

RICHARD

Really….

CHESTER

It's gonna blow your mind!

OLLIE

You see, we know what it was like. We were across the ocean once upon a time – in America. Either sweating at a factory making crap money, or running from the noose in the south, or biding time in the jail, like my main man here.

CHESTER

See, the setting's in Harlem – you got this real slick brother, who's got some biiiiig money coming in from a Joe Louis fight..

Four Men in Paris

OLLIE
Chester Himes. Chester grew up in Harlem, just like his many dime novel heroes. Colorful, bright, pugilistic and full of ideas. Stuff Hollywood would have eaten up – and actually did, til Jack Warner of the Warner Brothers found out he was black and kicked him out. But you can't stop the dreamer – not here in Paris..

RICHARD
You told me about this one, Chester – you shot that by me last week..

CHESTER
No, I made some twists...check out the chick I wrote about...

OLLIE
Of course all of us budding writers were trying to make it – trying to climb up to that great Everest-ic mountain top. The one Richard ascended. He was the master of us all. Serene, majestic, a publisher of three great literary masterpieces. Everyone heard of Native Son, that one novel that lit a torch that illuminated black writing to the eyes of all, black and white. Black Boy, his autobiography that really grabbed the nastiness of the south and what it meant growing up a nigger and put it right under the readers' noses – no matter how it stunk. Uncle Tom's Children was my favorite – the collection of short stories – snapshots of black life, that no one knew except those of us who lived it. That's what Richard brought to us..

RICHARD
Hey Ollie!

OLLIE
And that's what he was trying to pass down to us – his "disciples"

RICHARD
Didn't you hear this crap from Chester yesterday?

OLLIE
[coming to the table, joining the men] Man, you guys starting up already? It's 6am!

CHESTER
So?

OLLIE
Other people'r trying to eat!

CHESTER
Richard – so this chick got a loan from this other brother.

RICHARD
Lemme guess – she's got herself into a world of trouble and it's up to the brother to get her out of it, right?

CHESTER
Well, see on page 3..

RICHARD
Man, I heard that same crap so many times! Formulaic stuff you got from Hollywood..

CHESTER
This is a pulp novel..

RICHARD
It's toilet paper! You can wipe your ass on that –

OLLIE
[watching the other patrons] Folks are talking..

RICHARD

So? Let em talk. **[smiling]** Isn't that the point? To get em talking. But about what? Dime novels? Or something serious? Something concrete? Something people can use in their lives? Something to help our people rise up from where they are? Tell me, man, what are people gonna learn from that?

CHESTER

You haven't even read it.

RICHARD

You've got more talent than that, brother. Haven't I taught you brothers at least one thing: your words can start a revolution! You can inject consciousness with your writings. You can be Voltaire, you can be Martin Luther and start a movement. A blank piece of paper can chart your destiny and those who read it – depending on what you write.

CHESTER

[resigned] Richard, do me a favor and read the paper. Save the speech for Jimmy.

OLLIE

Yeah, your pupil.

RICHARD

That goddamned Judas **(all laugh)** I'm serious. Did you see what he wrote…

CHESTER

Wait a minute now – now if he's Judas, then you are…

OLLIE

Yup

RICHARD
No, I'm not saying *that*…

OLLIE
Sounds like it to me..

CHESTER
You stepped in it this time, my man!

OLLIE
Hey – lemme touch the helm of your garment..

RICHARD
Yeah, and heal y'all fools' dirty minds **[all laugh]**

CHESTER
Ok, so where is the prodigal son of yours?

RICHARD
I think I see him…

CHESTER
And what's this shit about him getting locked up? The desk clerk who wrote the message can't write worth a God damn..

RICHARD
[looking at a distance] Yup, that's him.

OLLIE
Jimmy, is of course, James Baldwin. The youngest of all of us – newly arrived in the City of Dreams. Jimmy was a young buck, a writer full of nervous energy and a searing desire to be accepted – well, hell, I guess all of us went through that when we were kids. Needing a pat on the head from dear ol' Dad.

JAMES
[carrying his suitcase, looking weary and sleepily] Hey fellas..

CHESTER
God damn, Jimmy – what hole did you drag yourself out of?

JAMES
Shoot – jail's rough, man. I'm sure Richard told you..

RICHARD
[to chester] You know this boy? Who is this boy?

CHESTER [with Ollie giggling]
Aw, stop it Richard.

RICHARD
[mimicking a white cracker] Where you from boy? You ain't from these parts..

JAMES
[unsure of how to play with the joke] Uh, sir, well.. oh, come on Richard..

RICHARD
Watchu say, boy? Hey, you see a colored sign around here, boy?

OLLIE
HAH! Sounds just like the whities back south, don't he?

CHESTER
Ok, Richard, you can cut it out – have a seat, Jimmy

RICHARD
WHAT!! Sit here? We're dignified white folk – what'chu talking about? [all roar in laughter. Richard drops the act, throws an envelope at Jimmy]. There you go.

JAMES
What's this?

RICHARD
Some francs. They took your money, right?

JAMES
Well they gave me back my suitcases..

RICHARD
..but whatever you had in your pockets or laying around in the hotel, they confiscated, right? So you're busted, you need money and there you go. This is so you won't have to bullshit me for a half hour, tell me how wonderful I am, and then hit me up for money.

JAMES
Uh.. well.. **[scoops the envelope and stuffs it in his pocket]** I do need it. Thanks, Richard.

CHESTER
Slow up. How did you get busted?

JAMES
So I got here yesterday around this time. And, like, I meet some folks – you know the folks, who wrote me while I was in the states, they're gonna publish my latest article..

OLLIE
C'mon man – get to it..

JAMES
Well there was this guy who was there.. sort of a bougoise type.. well I wouldn't say that..

Four Men in Paris

                    CHESTER
Uh, James…

                    JAMES
Well he approached me around the evening.. I'd say..

                    RICHARD
Basically, they say you stole some sheets.

                    CHESTER
What?

                    RICHARD
Yup. Sheets. Crime of the century, really.

                    CHESTER
You got busted for stealing sheets?

                    JAMES
Well we were asked to move from one hotel suite to another..

                    RICHARD
..and you took the sheets from the first suite to the 2nd.

                    JAMES
And that's stealing??

                    CHESTER
Ok. Basically, the cops were fucking with you.

                    RICHARD
Well there's also the gentleman… right?

                    JAMES
The gentleman?

Four Men in Paris

CHESTER
Yeah. This "bougois type" .. who was this guy?

JAMES
Well he was just .. this guy.. harmless, really..

RICHARD
James, james, james.. when are you gonna learn?

JAMES
It wasn't like that.. but let's change the subject.

OLLIE
[laughes] Good idea

JAMES
There's someone I want all of us to meet..

CHESTER
[joking] Well if it's this bougois guy, you can count me out.. I'm not into that type of stuff

JAMES
No, no – this is a publisher who's interested in black writers.

RICHARD
Yes – I can see that! **[all laugh]**

JAMES
No.. c'mon you guys, listen to me..

OLLIE
We all had fun picking on James, who's KNOWN for getting himself into precarious situations. Of course, James was in the closet – he wanted to put up a good front for us, but we knew. And to be honest, we didn't care – he can be whatever he wants

Four Men in Paris

and be with whomever he wants. All of us could. Chester's been dating a couple of really sexy Parisian women and having the time of his life. Richard was always dutiful, pining away on his novels with his wife and child by his side. Me – well I'm not putting my stuff out there. The uptight citizens in Paris were calling the cops, wanting them to enforce morality laws, but we weren't gonna let our man James stew in county jail. We were free black men in this most wonderful city. Paris. And James took us to a really swank party with some publishers – who had money to spend..

****

ACT TWO Scene 2 – the Party.

CHESTER, FATIMA, JAMES, OLLIE, RICHARD are at MARIGOLD'S house for drinks. Another socialite guy is there, perhaps Sartre. Everyone is a bit tipsy.

RICHARD
So explain to me this article..

JAMES
Richard, you have it all wrong..

MARIGOLD
It didn't seem off-colored to me..

JAMES
I'm simply saying that we've evolved – as writers and as black people. Listen, Native Son was a masterpiece. At its time, it was exactly what we needed. It perfectly explored the black consciousness..

RICHARD
Don't kiss my ass, Jimmy. Bigger is the 20th century Uncle Tom??

CHESTER
Now Richard, I don't think he was saying ..

RICHARD
Did you read it? That's what he's saying. Do I look like Harriet Beecher Stowe? **(everyone laughs)** I look like a white woman to you?

Four Men in Paris

FATIMA
Who's Harriet Beecher Stowe?

CHESTER
She wrote Uncle Tom's Cabin, back in 1852.

OLLIE
Horrible book.

JEAN
Oh, it wasn't that bad. Didn't it start the whole abolitionist movement?

OLLIE
Well, sure..

RICHARD
No, it didn't. There were plenty of movements and abolitionists going on around that time – Tubman, Frederick Douglass, Quincy Adams, the Barnburners, the Republican party..

MARIGOLD
But didn't Lincoln say this was the little woman that started the big war?

RICHARD
(indignant) And?

JAMES
Yes, that was her. And it was a decent book for the time. That's my point, Richard. Uncle Tom has his time. Native Son had his time. And now it's time..

RICHARD
For who? You? Ok, James – where's your masterpiece? Show us your novel!

JEAN
Well James has a wonderful piece we're publishing in the …

RICHARD
I'm not talking about essays, or critiques. Anybody can put together a couple of paragraphs. I'm talking about books – real books! That's what I don't understand about you, Jimmy. A brother helps a brother out getting overseas, getting him situated in Paris, bailing him out of jail and not only do you write this crap, but I had to hear about it from Chester! You couldn't even tell me yourself.

JAMES
I was gonna tell you.. **(reaction from the fellas)** But listen - I'm trying to help pave the way for new writers. You can't expect writers like us to copy from you, Richard. I mean Bigger Thomas – he's a big, ugly, uneducated – you can't even call him a man, even – and he savagely kills a young white woman..

CHESTER
.. and his black girlfriend..

OLLIE
You better stay out of it –

JAMES
Now how does that uplift the black race? How can Bigger Thomas be a cornerstone for black people? What redeeming quality does Bigger have?

MARIGOLD
You have to admit, he's got a point, Richard.

RICHARD **(quiet, stewing)**
That's not the question. The question is: who made him? Who created him?

Four Men in Paris

JEAN
Right – the white establishment.

JAMES
Actually, YOU created him, Richard. Think about it –

RICHARD
Wait a minute! I created the situation that created Bigger Thomas?? I created Jim Crow? I wrote the laws that's held back the black race for the last hundred years??

JAMES
That's not my point –

OLLIE
I think what Jimmy's saying –

CHESTER
(laughing) Lord – ok, folks, let's all calm down – we all getting loud –

RICHARD
Read the book again, Jimmy! Bigger is the product of racism and prejudice. Hell, we're ALL Bigger Thomas – we've all gone through what he's gone through! All of us a product of the hatred we've been subjected to – Bigger is just spitting out what's been spat on him through the years!

JAMES
(exhausted) Richard, no one wants to hear that story **(Richard laughs out loud)** – listen – Native Son is about the ugliness of the black man. I'm not Bigger Thomas. I'm not. I'm educated. I have love in my heart.

Four Men in Paris

RICHARD
(sarcastically) That's wonderful, Jimmy. We're all happy for you.

JAMES
And the world should see the black man not as an ape or this monster leashed on society. But as a dignified, established man of the world. A man like you. Chester. Ollie. Me. You understand now?

RICHARD
(looks at his glass) I need another shot.

CHESTER
(Takes the glass from Richard) I think you've had enough, partner. Look, Jimmy's trying to establish himself – hell we all are. Me – Langston Hughes..

RICHARD
Oh, shit. That pickaninny –

OLLIE **(roars laughing)**
Wow – called the man a pickanniny!

CHESTER
Well the man's trying..

RICHARD **(mocking Langston)**
Lissen, chil' an' I's tell you

RICHARD and OLLIE
Life for me ain't no crystal stair! **(all laugh)**

RICHARD
Because apparently, all black folk talk like that..

Four Men in Paris

JAMES
Well you did the same thing in your book, Richard. Uncle Tom's Children..

RICHARD
No, that's subverting the language to address the situation, not embracing it! God, do I have to explain everything?

CHESTER
We get your point. But Langston trying to get paid, just like us. It sold, right?

RICHARD
That's the goal?

CHESTER
Money's what it's all about my friend. That's the thing.

JAMES
No, I wouldn't say that – it's about –

RICHARD
It's about the voice. Your words on paper is a voice! What are you saying? Are you whispering, or shouting? I coulda wasted my time writing pleasant shit people wanted to hear. To *appease* people.. that's not the point..

JAMES (to his white friends)
I can never win these arguments..

RICHARD
You have to yell! You have to scream! To agitate! Your words must have life! That's what the people need. Let them see the ugliness they created! You can't make change by pacifying people –

JAMES
Richard, ok.. ok.. you win.

RICHARD
And don't try to pacify me either! Jimmy – your words must have meaning.

JAMES
They do! To me! You say I shouldn't pacify you but every goddamn time I write something, you shit all over me. I say it has meaning and you say it don't. So when will it have meaning – when YOU say so?

RICHARD
(taken aback) Well if that's how you feel – you don't have to listen to me.

JEAN
Do you mind if I intervene?

OLLIE
Please do.

JEAN
This has been a wonderful little debate, but aren't we all talking about validity? Existence? Aren't we all trying to define ourselves?

RICHARD **(solemnly)**
I don't have that problem. I've already defined myself..

JEAN
And your book sales solidifies your definition, which was Chester's point – Chester, right? **(Chester acknowledges).** I'm a writer, too, Richard. And I'm defined by what I write and who reads it and how it changes them. But which comes first? My

reaction to them or their reaction to me? Am I defined by my outside environments – by a government who will dictate what I buy, what taxes I pay and what's done with the money and what restrictions they put on me? Or will I have the courage to define *myself* on my own terms – where I set my own rules..

RICHARD
I think we're getting a little off track here..

JEAN
No, stay with me. Your Jim Crow was my National Socialist tormentors several years ago. We all have masters, don't we? Imperialistic "fathers" dictating our every move. And we have a choice. We either obey and receive our desserts for our obedience. Or we resist – and go in the great unknown and bear the cross of independence. Of being different.

RICHARD
Thank you! That's my point – exactly – the cross..

MARIGOLD (to JEAN)
And I thought you were atheist..

RICHARD
You bear the cross and I'm writing about the cross! Bigger's carrying the cross of his fourfathers, and his explosion, his anger..

JEAN
Actually, I was making James' point.

RICHARD
His.. what?

JAMES
You were?

JEAN
Yes. You see, Richard, you are the imperialistic father. James is the son. And to exist, the son must destroy the father.

(All pause – laughter erupts from everyone except the man and Fatima)

RICHARD | OLLIE | CHESTER | JAMES (simultaneously)
What the fuck! / Oh boy, I need a refill / Uh, whoa! Ok, who's the mom? / Ok, that didn't help…

RICHARD
How the hell am I the father?

JEAN
Well, let's examine – James is your protégé, and has depended on you for literary feedback and for finances..

JAMES
Well, a little bit.

CHESTER, RICHARD and OLLIE
Naw, you got it right..

JEAN
But he's written an article that diminishes your finest work and uplifts him in a new light. What better way to define his independence as a young man and a writer than to publicly destroy you?

JAMES
Jean, you can stop now. In any case, Marigold is a publisher and I think she can help out with..

Four Men in Paris

RICHARD
Wait – is he right? You need to destroy me to uplift yourself?

JEAN
Don't be ashamed, James. All you wrote were words. You men are grown enough to handle constructive criticism..

RICHARD
(mockingly) Yeah. Don't worry.. daddy won't take off the belt **(chuckles from Chester and Ollie)**

CHESTER
Hey y'all, I want to introduce to you a wonderful lady I had to pleasure of meeting...

(JAMES storms out of the apartment)

MARIGOLD
James – James – oh no.

RICHARD
Let him go – he'll cool off.

OLLIE
This happens all the time.

CHESTER
So this is Fatima. Fatima, Richard – Ollie..

OLLIE
So what do you think of the discussion? Of existence?

JEAN
Yes, do you define yourself or does the world define you?

FATIMA
Well – uh, my English is not great. So I don't understand a lot of what was said. I don't know.

CHESTER
Well I define her as one FIIIIIIINE Hot lady!

FATIMA **(blushing)**
I use the bathroom. **(exits)**

OLLIE
Man, you robbing the cradle, ain't you?

CHESTER
What you mean?? She's in her 20's!

MARIGOLD **(to JEAN)**
Jean, I think you were too blunt with James.

JEAN
Really? I think I was only exposing what was already there.

RICHARD
He's right. Very enlightening. Don't worry about it.

CHESTER
"I won't take off the belt" - Dick, man I think you're crazy!

RICHARD
Why?

CHESTER
You're like Jeckyll and Hyde – one moment, you're so cultured, and then you go nuts! Saying shit that runs people off.

Four Men in Paris

RICHARD
So you like your gin with soda – watered down?

CHESTER
No, you know I can handle it straight.

RICHARD
The boy needs to grow up. He can give it but he can't take it.

CHESTER
He just wrote an essay..

RICHARD
…to appease white people.

CHESTER
To me, sounds like he's trying to reach a younger black generation.

RICHARD
(pointing to JEAN) You're just as bad as this dude is! Why don't you tuck him in and read him a bedtime story!

CHESTER
The boy's gotta find his own voice –

RICHARD
(turning away) Like you? – writing dime novels..

OLLIE
Look out, he's after you now.

CHESTER
(to MARIGOLD) what did you put in his drink? **(FATIMA gestures to CHESTER that she wants to go)**

RICHARD
No, I'm serious – what kind of enlightenment anyone's getting from these ridiculous stories about some black hustler in Harlem and who he's nickle' and dim'in?

CHESTER
Who says everyone needs to be enlightened all the time?

RICHARD
Chester, you know you can do better. If you applied that writing, the way I did in Heart of Darkness –

CHESTER (holding his hand to a "stop")
Richard – I'm not Jimmy. You're not my father **(pats DICK on the shoulder).** I need a smoke break. **(exits with Fatima)**

RICHARD
(playfully to JEAN) You started this! **(phone rings)**

MARIGOLD
Yes, he's here. Richard?

RICHARD (yells to the phone)
I'll be home in an hour.

MARIGOLD
Yes, I'll tell him. **(hangs up)** I think she wants you home now.

RICHARD
(checks watch) Yeah, I know. **(to Ollie)** Am I that bad?

OLLIE
What' you mean?

Four Men in Paris

                    RICHARD
James. And Chester. Am I that bad? I'm good to a brother, ain't I?

                     OLLIE
Dick, you give em the truth, whether they like it or not. **(OLLIE steps out of the scene while behind him, the scene changes).**

****

ACT ONE, Scene 3. Ollie smoothly transitions out of scene while continuously talking.

Chester had it the best out of all of us. Didn't matter how many grey hairs he was pushing up, he could still catch the ladies. An ex-boxer who mauled his way out of Brooklyn, he had that chiseled physique all of us envied, even Richard. He had the knowledge of an old saint but the body of a young boy in heat. It both fascinated and intimidated that little fawn, Fatima..

FATIMA's laughter is heard while SL goes dark and SR brightens up on CHESTER chasing FATIMA along a street – basically an open SR area with perhaps street signs along the back wall

FATIMA
Chester, you're crazy!

CHESTER
Of course I am, for you.

FATIMA
Why?

CHESTER
What do you mean why?

FATIMA
What do you like about me? What about me makes you crazy?

CHESTER
(French accent) Your hair, your eyes, your body..

FATIMA
You make fun of me..

CHESTER
No.. that's my French accent – like those charming French men..

FATIMA
Chester, if I thought French men were charming, I wouldn't be with you now.

CHESTER
You're so sweet **(he kisses her – Chester wants more, but Fatima pulls away)**

FATIMA
So what's wrong with your friends – they're so angry!

CHESTER
Naw, that's just how we are – passionate writers, strong opinions..

FATIMA
That Richard, he's scary!

CHESTER
Dick's ok. He's just intense. You ever read his books?

FATIMA
No.. I read yours only. I show it to my mom – she don't like it. C'est sale.

CHESTER
Sa-lay? Uh.. dirty?

FATIMA
Yes. Too dirty! You're learning!

CHESTER
What, the love scenes?

FATIMA

Yeah, she don't like that. She says dirty mind writes these things.

CHESTER

That's just passion.

FATIMA
(Turns away from Chester, who walks slowly behind her)
Well I think there's too much. The woman – you describe how the man feels up her dress, clutches her, fondles her, kisses and licks in her ear, saying those words, and…

CHESTER
(Tries to fondle Fatima)
Yes…..

FATIMA

You distract me, Chester. I'm trying to talk.

CHESTER

I'm distracted, too.

FATIMA
(Turns to Chester) You must calm yourself, Chester. We have time.

CHESTER

We have time right now. Why wait?

FATIMA

I'm not ready. Not right now.

CHESTER

What's the problem? I know you want me.. **(Unbuttons his shirt to reveal his chest)**

Four Men in Paris

FATIMA

Chester, we're in the street!

CHESTER

And we're alone. I've seen you look at me. No need to hold back, Fatima. Here.. touch me.

FATIMA

Chester, I think we're good friends. Very close. We should be closer..

CHESTER
(Perplexed)

Uh, yeah.. I'm trying to get closer..

FATIMA

(Searching for the English word) I mean closer in the mind. In the heart. Not flesh. We should wait.

CHESTER

(Frustrated) I don't understand. We're not kids. You're not a kid anymore, Fatima. You don't have to worry about disobeying your mom. Just relax.

FATIMA

(Insulted) And I don't worry about disobeying you. It's late. I have to go. I go alone.

CHESTER

Awww, c'mon. Fatima. Hey..

OLLIE

My daddy once said "A woman's like a butterfly – beautiful winged creatures that blossom in the spring. But you gotta close your hands quick – or they fly away". Beautiful analogy, though I don't know how right it is – maybe that's a man's problem –

Four Men in Paris

always trying to close his hands too quick and not let things happen naturally. Though, sometimes…

(Out of the shadows of USR comes VELVET, a sultry woman who had observed the entire FATIMA/CHESTER scene)

The butterfly flies right in your hands – without you doing a thing at all.

VELVET
(Imitating FATIMA) No, Ches-TER, I go home.. you touch too much.. oh my god Ches-TER, you touch my boobies, I tell my mama…

CHESTER
(Laughing) Yeah, very funny.

VELVET
Who knows, maybe a year from now, you can get to touch her knees!

CHESTER
(Weakly defending FATIMA) well, it is getting late.

VELVET
My friend, it's always late. Blink your eye, the moment is gone! Too late. You wanted a kiss but you wait. Blink – she's gone! Too late. You want to get her number. You blink – she's gone. She get off the bus. Too late. It is ALWAYS late.

CHESTER
Yup.

VELVET

You want something, you get it. Now. **(Takes out an unlit cigarette)**

CHESTER

Very true.

VELVET

(Pauses – clears her throat) I need to give you a hint?

CHESTER

Where are my manners? **(offers to light her cigarette)**

VELVET

(Takes the lighter from him) Manners don't mean nothing. Never waste an opportunity. Velvet.

CHESTER

What?

VELVET

(Pause) My name. Velvet. I thought you brothers were more on top of it!

CHESTER

You just caught me by surprise.

VELVET

Did I? **(Beat – she looks him over, checks the clothing)** How long you been here, in France?

CHESTER

Couple of years.

VELVET
(Walks to Chester – places both her hands on his jacket, his shirt, feels him up – then puts out her cigarette) Nice. Rue La Merge?

CHESTER
Hmm?

VELVET
Your clothing. You get this from Rue La Merge?

CHESTER
Think so, can't remember the shop.

VELVET
You can do better. But with a nice body, doesn't really matter, does it? **(Chester chuckles)** Awww, now who's being shy?

CHESTER
So how about you? I take it you're a native? **(VELVET just looks at him)** Where are you from?

VELVET
Everywhere and no where. All at the same time.

CHESTER
Mysterious. **(Velvet plays with Chester's nose)** You're screwing with me.

VELVET
Maybe. But I do it well, don't I? **(Both laugh)** Well if we're going to **(Pause)** chit-chat, then we'd better go inside.

CHESTER
Oh.

Four Men in Paris

VELVET
(Offers arm) Well, I'm following you. This can be a special night, "Ches-TER". **(Serious)** Depending on what you can bring to the table. **(Both leave to go to Chester's apartment)**

OLLIE
Ches-TER!! Haha, fun-ny. Love that. Yeah, Velvet was a pistol! She was a wild one and for a while, Chester had a lot of fun with her. Where Chester was a rock, James was a feather. **(Notices James)** Poor James – a black writer in a white man's world, and an outcast even to his own people. Who would be there for James…?

(A handsome waiter, FRANCOIS, appears)

FRANCOIS
Would you like a refresher?

JAMES
Thanks, no.

FRANCOIS
Just let me know what else you need… Mister Baldwin.

JAMES
(Raises his head) You know me?

FRANCOIS
Go Tell It On The Mountain? Notes of a Native Son? Oui, I know you very well. **(Pause)** I mean, I don't know you. I know your work.

JAMES
Yes.

Four Men in Paris

FRANCOIS
But I could… know you. Get to know you.

JAMES
Yes. You a writer too?

FRANCOIS
Well, I used to. I lost the spirit. I don't have the talent. But I read. Poetry, novels, things.

JAMES
Yes.

FRANCOIS
You know the works of Dumas? The son and the father?

JAMES
(Hits a nerve) uh, yes.

FRANCOIS
I love their works. Great black writers. In the Victorian age, even. **(pause)** I have all their works, at my flat. It's actually upstairs, just above this café, the 2nd floor. We could…

JAMES
Uh, no. Sorry. **(Pays for drinks, scurries off)**

OLLIE
Or rather, who would James *allow* to be there for him?

Four Men in Paris

****

ACT ONE, Scene 4

Ollie speaks once again to the audience, center stage. Directly behind him (and hopefully, throughout the **FATIMA/CHESTER/VELVET** scene), Upstage center has transformed into **RICHARD's** apartment – center should be a dining room table, similar or exactly like the table used in I:2; the kitchen is SL and Richard's mini office is SR. **JULIA's** play area is downstage SL, in front of the kitchen but that can be established by small rug brought on by **JULIA**, after Ollie's mini monologue. **ELLEN** is taking dishes from the CS table to the kitchen and washing them.

OLLIE
Ah, I can remember those days when I ran around, back when you didn't have a care in the world! Shoot, I got two kids back in the states, so every bit of dough I get – from selling political comics to newspapers – some of that money's going back home. Now my old woman and I are done – maybe I'll get married again, maybe not, who knows. Now Dick and Ellen have been around for at least a decade. Hmm. You'd think marriage would be all heaven. In the beginning it is, of course. But you really know what a true love is all about, when you can endure the hell. Together.

RICHARD
You guys are still up?

ELLEN
Yes we are.

JULIA
You're late, Dad.

RICHARD
Yes, I know.

JULIA
Mom, is the cake ready?

ELLEN
No. It has to stay in the oven for an hour. And don't stomp around in the kitchen – the cake won't rise.

JULIA
Cake rises?

ELLEN
Yes. The baking soda has what you call sodium bicarbonate. Causes little bubbles to form and make the cake rise.

JULIA
Huh?

ELLEN
Never mind.

JULIA
Mom's upset.

ELLEN
No I'm not.

JULIA
You said Dad should have ..

ELLEN
Julia! How's your homework doing?

JULIA
I'm done – here (presents Ellen with her homework)

RICHARD
Did Paul call?

ELLEN
No, he didn't. That's good, sweetie. Time for bed.

JULIA
Can't I stay up for a bit? It's Friday.

ELLEN
Your dad and I need to talk.

RICHARD
Uh oh.

JULIA
Good night Dad. (kisses and hugs Richard) You're in trouble. (exits)

RICHARD
I'm in trouble.

ELLEN
Don't listen to her. (kiss) But I was a little upset.

RICHARD
What now?

ELLEN
Why didn't you invite me?

RICHARD
Where?

ELLEN
This thing you went to. This party. Who's Marigold?

RICHARD
One of Jimmy's friends. She's a publisher for this magazine – that's who he's working for.

ELLEN
Good. He can start paying us back.

RICHARD
Ellen..

ELLEN
Richard, I don't want to nag, but we're trying to budget. We only have 5,000,000 francs left in our account. We can't afford to bail your friends out of jail.

RICHARD
I'd argue we can't afford NOT to bail our brothers out of jail. You think me, a black man, would let my brother stay in jail, knowing I can free him?

ELLEN
And Marigold couldn't bail him out?

RICHARD
Yes, she could. And she didn't. Hellova commentary on the state of the world and race relations, isn't it?

Four Men in Paris

ELLEN
I could say the same thing about Paul. He was supposed to call you?

RICHARD
Yeah. I sent my last manuscript out to him last week and he's supposed to give me the good word.

ELLEN
And give you an advance.

RICHARD
Ellen, we're doing ok. Ok, I'll watch our spending. I promise. I think you worry too much.

ELLEN
Well, that's all I do these days, is watch our spending. (sighs) I need to get back into writing. You think Marigold can publish some of my stuff?

RICHARD
You can't do that and take care of Rachel at the same time.

ELLEN
Sure I can.

RICHARD
It's not a good idea. It's been years since you wrote anything.

ELLEN
Yes. I wonder why's that.

RICHARD
It's my fault?

ELLEN
I gave up a part of myself – my career as a writer, an activist, fighting for equality for women and minorities – I was a part of that front line. But I put a ring on my finger and said I do.. to you.

RICHARD
Would you like a refund?

ELLEN
I don't mean it like that. (sits on Richard's lap) I wanna go away, sometimes…

RICHARD
We have our summer cottage in England.

ELLEN
No, I mean home.

RICHARD
To America?

ELLEN
Yes. I miss my parents. I miss the language. I miss Nathan's hot dogs. Don't you? (Richard walks away) Julia and Rachel should experience the USA – they're Americans.

RICHARD
I'm never going back to that hellhole.

ELLEN
Richard, you're being harsh.

RICHARD
I am? You know what I had to endure – the bullshit down south, your friends in New York..

ELLEN
Richard, that was 13 years ago. Things have changed – things are progressing over there. Haven't you read about the movement and the works of Dr. King..

RICHARD
Ellen, please –

ELLEN
Okay, I won't talk about it anymore.

RICHARD
There's more to the world than the USA. Like Ghana.

ELLEN
Yes. And you're going back there, again?

RICHARD
It's their third anniversary. I'll be quick – I have to give a speech.

ELLEN
Are they paying your way?

RICHARD
Yes, they're covering it.
ELLEN
And try not to piss anyone off there. You know papers in the states are following you..

RICHARD

I know. That's why I do it. I'm an agitator. You don't make change unless you stir the pot. (holds her) I thought that's why you married me.

ELLEN

I understand the struggle, Richard. You are an agitator. But you're also a husband and a father. (kiss) You have enemies out there. But not here. You have family here.

RICHARD

(puzzled) I know that.

ELLEN

I'm just reminding you. I may fuss, Richard, but I'm not the enemy. I want what's best for all of us.

RICHARD

What's this all about?

ELLEN

I just want to make sure you see me as your wife. Your partner. Someone who loves you.

RICHARD

Ellen, don't be silly.

ELLEN

I don't know about you sometimes. The Outsider? Savage Holiday? You have your main characters killing women...

RICHARD

Ellen, the stories are deeper than that.

ELLEN

I think that's why Paul is having a hard time publishing them.

RICHARD
What do you want me to do? Keep writing books like Native Son? Black Boy?

ELLEN
They sold. They were successful.

RICHARD
That was over 15 years ago.

ELLEN
Well, look at Chester's books.. (sees a change in Richard) Richard, can't I even talk to you anymore? I'm not trying to hurt you. You deserve success. People still look up to you. But.. it's been a long time since you were in America. You've been away from the very people you've been writing about. I just don't want you to lose yourself in Paris.

RICHARD
Frankly, I don't mind being lost in Paris. I'm being stonewalled in America because of those pricks in the US Government. Like those senators that said Black Boy was obscene. They want to stop me, to stop my writing. It won't work. Paul won't let them, and I won't let them. But that's not for you to worry about (hugs her) Listen, Paris is my freedom. I can write freely, I can breathe freely. No black only signs. No dealing with southern cops. No bowing my head and saying Yes suh. Look at me, Ellen. This is a free man – I haven't been able to say that in years. Free. Free to live, free to love. You understand?

ELLEN
Loud and clear. I should have known better than to debate you on how to write. Ok, let me clean these plates. But let me know what Paul says. When are you leaving for Ghana?

RICHARD

Next week.

ELLEN

I'll make sure you're packed. Richard, no more loaning money to Jimmy.

RICHARD

You're worrying about money again. What did I tell you?

ELLEN

You make the money, I make the home. I'll hold you to that, Richard.

****

ACT TWO, Scene 1. Morning. There should be a musical interlude as the lights fade on Richard and Ellen – in the blue lighting, the stage hands will change the set as if they're dancing, while Ollie comes back to DSC and addresses the audience. When he finishes, behind him should be CHESTER's apartment – basically the center should be the bed – a dresser SR and the bathroom where RICHARD's kitchen was.

OLLIE

Two people trying to put it together is rough, sometimes – some of you out there know what I mean, don't you? Well, Ellen had to hold on those francs as hard as she could – and hold on to Richard's dreams. I wonder – how hard is it to believe in someone's else dream? Especially when you're asked to forgo your own dreams? Speaking of dreams, good ol' Chester sure nuff got his dream – course last night, I don't think he did a lot of dreaming, know what I mean? Oh, yeah, that hot fox Velvet gave him the night of his life. **(starts to start off stage, but doubles back)** Y'now what my dad always said? "Boy, there two kinds of gifts in life. One is by God, and one is by the Devil. You may get the gift you want, but who's giving it to you?" God? Satan? You ever think about that? I'm sure Chester didn't give it no mind either..

CHESTER

(Both he and VELVET are in bed) Oh, wow.. what time is it.

VELVET
(Velvet laughs)

It's too late

CHESTER

Huh?

Four Men in Paris

VELVET
You don't get the joke? You're not very quick, Chester?

CHESTER
Well at 7am, I'm not that quick..

VELVET
You weren't quick last night either.. which is a good thing. **(CHESTER looks at VELVET, who breaks out into laughter)** You don't get that either? Aw, poor Chester.

CHESTER
(teases VELVET) but I got it last night, didn't I?

VELVET
(snuggles with him) Yes, you did. You were very good. No.. you were very BAD!

CHESTER
Wasn't I?

VELVET
(goes to imaginary mirror, admires herself) You know, a good relationship is nothing without chemistry.

CHESTER
Of course.

VELVET
Of course, eh? Lotta people don't know that. Lotta people think – oh, if we talk to one another, if I get to know his mind, his thoughts, things will be ok. That's bullshit. It's chemistry. Sexual chemistry. Chemicals in the body. The stuff that burns inside you. You don't have nobody that makes you burn inside, you got nothing.

Four Men in Paris

CHESTER
(Walks up behind her, snuggling her)
Yeah, I hear you.

VELVET
Yeah, and you feel me too. **(kiss)** You make me burn inside, Chester. We're wild, like tigers. Carnal. I can feel it. Can't you?

CHESTER
There's definitely something there.

VELVET
(a beat) Something wrong?

CHESTER
No.

VELVET
Don't bullshit me. What is it?

CHESTER
I know nothing about you.

VELVET
Why you care? What difference does it make? I tell you about my ma, my pop, I tell you where I grew up, that I play with dolls as a kid, what pet I had, who hurt me in the past, what does it matter? I don't tell you about my past because it's irrelevant. It's about now – **(grabs his hands and has him clutch her)** this is real. This is the only thing that's real, right now. My life is not what was, but what I make it.

CHESTER
Just like writing a book.

VELVET

Right, just like one of your novels. **(jumps on the bed, picks up some of CHESTER's papers from the side table)** That's what I love about you. **(takes a blank piece of paper, twirls it around like a wand or a cape).** You take a blank piece of paper, and create a whole world from it – a universe where people can escape and live a new life, even for a moment. I read some of your stuff, while you sleep. You have talent. You sexy, talented, gifted black man, you.

CHESTER

Compliments, compliments.

VELVET

And I want to be your muse.

CHESTER

My muse?

VELVET

Your inspiration – I want to be the mystery woman you write about – that vixen men drool and crave for, especially at night. You write about me, Chester? Please?

(A knock at the door)

VELVET

Don't tell them I'm here. Please.

CHESTER

Who? **(Another knock; CHESTER goes to the door – downstage, invisible; and an French police officer is there)** Yes, can I help you?

Four Men in Paris

OFFICER
You are Chester Himes?

CHESTER
Yes. A problem?

OFFICER
(Comes in the scene – Velvet is under the bed, hiding) You were with a woman tonight?

CHESTER
(Pause) uh, yes.

OFFICER
We're looking for her. You will give us her location.

CHESTER
Well, I can write down Fatima's address – she's about a half mile from here – you'd have to walk away from the Champs Elysee..

OFFICER
Fatima?

CHESTER
Yes, young girl, in her 20's – here's a picture of her. **(Shows OFFICER picture from side table)**

OFFICER
No, this isn't the lady.

CHESTER
That's who I was with last night.

OFFICER
No one else?

Four Men in Paris

CHESTER
Who are you looking for?

OFFICER
(Looks around the apartment; CHESTER sits on the bed) There is a lady who is a fugitive from justice. I can't get into the details of the case, it's still pending. But I don't have to remind you, Mister Himes, that it's a felony to harbor a criminal.

CHESTER
Of course.

OFFICER
You American black fellows have made a real impression in this part of Paris – I know you write books and that's fine and all, but the parties, the shenanigans – and one of you was jailed two days ago for indecent exposure. There are people in this community that do NOT like your influence.

CHESTER
Really?

OFFICER
I'm only warning you, Mister Himes. You have your freedoms here in Paris, but do not abuse them. People are watching you – all of you. Good day. **(Officer leaves. Velvet emerges US from under the bed)**

CHESTER
Now what..

VELVET
SSSHHHH.. **(VELVET goes to the SR stage to see and hear if the officer is gone).** Ok, we can talk.

Four Men in Paris

CHESTER
Yeah, so I'm listening. Tell me what's going on.

VELVET
Just a misunderstanding. They say I shoplift. Took some lipstick. Crazy.

CHESTER
You sure? Sounds more serious than that.

VELVET
Oh, it's nothing. Hey, I'm hungry. Let's go to the café. You hungry?

CHESTER
Wait a minute.. he came in here because you stole lipstick?

VELVET
They SAY I stole lipstick. It's nothing.

CHESTER
You sure?

VELVET
I told you what it is. You don't believe me?

CHESTER
Ok, if that's what you say?

VELVET
(Forcefully) Hey, you don't believe me, tell me now! **(beat)** I'm sorry Chester. I can't talk to you that way. I tell you Paris is no good. Oh, sure, you like it when you first come. You're a foreigner and you don't have to deal with crazy American laws. But just watch, if you try to be too different, too independent, you'll be an outcast too – just like me.

Four Men in Paris

CHESTER

Is that what you are?

VELVET

(Changes the subject) Oh, Chester – tell me about America! I hear they have buildings – all of them as big as the Eiffel Tower! And lots of shopping..

CHESTER

Well that's New York..

VELVET

And everyone has big trucks to drive! I wanna drive a truck! Vroom, vroom!

CHESTER

Velvet, is everything ok?

VELVET

(Frantic) I want to go to America – take me to the United States, Chester. You go back home, right?

CHESTER

I don't plan on it. This is home for me.

VELVET

You don't even speak the language!

CHESTER

(Tenderly) You can teach me.

VELVET

No – I want to go to America! Chester, I know you run away from some things. But that was a long time ago. Things are better now. You sell your books, people will see you differently. You're a made man now. Let's go back, together.

CHESTER

I'm not going back. And I'm running? Velvet, you're running. Just tell me what's going on. You can tell me. Why do the police want you?

VELVET

(Abrupt change) Nevermind. I have to go now. **(Hurriedly puts on clothes and goes to the door)** think about what I said. We can be wonderful together.

****

ACT TWO, Scene 2. The café, late morning. As Ollie talks, the bed, side table are removed and the café table is prominently center stage, as it was in I:1. RICHARD is there, drinking coffee and reading a paper.

OLLIE

Hmmm – what's going on there? Looks like Chester's got a WHOLE lot of stuff on his hands. Course, all he has to do is let that woman go and his troubles are over. But you know how we men are – am I right ladies? Now, while all THAT mess was going on, I met up with Dick in the morning. Dick was preparing for his trip to Ghana to celebrate their independence – but I think I threw a fly in his soup..

RICHARD

Your great leader, Kwame Nkruma, demanded independence at that United Gold Coast Convention several years ago, and on that day, he threw down the gauntlet. He drew the line. Oppression is finite, my brothers and sisters, but you must decide to draw the line. To end living in darkness. No man can be oppressed forever. Remember the agitation you caused against your oppressors.

OLLIE

Hmm...

RICHARD

What?

OLLIE

Nothing.

Four Men in Paris

RICHARD
C'mon man – that's what I use you as a sounding board. You'll give it to me straight. What's wrong with it?

OLLIE
Oppressors?

RICHARD
That's what they are..

OLLIE
You're talking about Europe – England..

RICHARD
Right. The country that held Ghana since 1874..

OLLIE
Oh, I know the history, Richard. I just don't know if you need to bring all that up again.

RICHARD
I'm not.

OLLIE
Well you mention oppression and oppressed two times already. And now you have agitation in there. I know you, Richard. You're winding up. You bout to let the whities have it.

RICHARD
I'm reminding my black brothers and sisters that they can't relax – to continue to fight for their freedom. To live in a democracy all their own.

OLLIE
I know where you're going, brother. But everyone's gonna be there. Vice President Nixon, English dignitaries, the press – it's

Four Men in Paris

an important speech for you. But I'm just saying you don't need to make any bad blood. Ghana has their freedom, they did it – it was a long, hard battle and they won. Leave it alone. I say keep the speech nice and pleasant. You can't walk into somebody's house party and start up old arguments..

RICHARD
You sound like Ellen.

OLLIE
You should listen to her.

RICHARD
Just back off? That's just what those dignitaries want, Ollie. That's just what the whities want. You of all people should know that!

OLLIE
You should listen to me.

RICHARD
I am, and I can't believe what I'm hearing. That's what's wrong with our people – the minute we're handed candy by our devils, we're mollified. We get passive.

OLLIE
Is that what I am? Mollified?

RICHARD
I don't mean you. You know what I'm talking about.

OLLIE
My man, how many devils can you fight? How many bricks are you going to throw? Richard, just because you're in Paris doesn't mean these devils can't strike you back. That passport is your lifeline – don't let them jam you up.

RICHARD
Oh, no. I'm not worried about that. France won't let that happen. We enhance France – they love us here.

OLLIE
Well just don't test the love too much. That's all I'm saying.

RICHARD
You worry too much. Hey, can I hit you up? I need a few francs before I go out of town. I'll pay you when I get back.

OLLIE
You have plenty of cash. That's what you told me last week.

RICHARD
(Sigh) I don't want Ellen to see any withdrawals from our account.

OLLIE
What about your publisher, Paul? You sent him that draft last week, right?

RICHARD
He says it needs work before I can get an advance.

OLLIE
Hmm.. that was that Island of whatever you call it..

RICHARD
Listen, do you have any money or not?

OLLIE
Sure, Richard, sure.. you know I'm always there for a brother. Yeah, I tried reading that draft of yours. Whew – a little.. cerebral for me. I don't' see the market for it.

RICHARD
I'm challenging their thinking – it's a new way to write, new concepts, it's abstract, but it's a way of identifying who we are and what we are as a people.

OLLIE
Hey, I can only give you 50,000 francs. If you want more, you should hit up Chester. He got a new advance yesterday.

RICHARD
It's really selling?

OLLIE
100,000 copies sold.

RICHARD
One hundred thousand. (lets it sink in) Hm.. well good for him. Brother's doing good.

OLLIE
He's heading over in a little bit. Let's all..

RICHARD
I gotta go. I gotta pack. (leaves) Uh, tell him I'm proud of him. Brother's doing good. (ruefully) Giving the people what they want. They want sugar water, give 'em sugar water. That's perfect.

OLLIE
Now Richard..

RICHARD
I'm going to do the REAL work. Someone's gotta do it.

Four Men in Paris

****

ACT TWO, Scene 3. A street

OLLIE

And there he goes – always the agitator. That was his mission. You see, Dick left America at a time where white supremacy was dominant and the black man had no answers. What Dick didn't know, or chose not to see, was that there was a growing movement going on right in the good ol' USA – where young black leaders were preparing a casket for good ol' Jimmy Crow. These young leaders were the successor of Bigger Thomas – the newer Native Sons.

JAMES

I hate to hit you up again..

CHESTER

.. yet here you are.

JAMES

Yeah, but..

CHESTER

Here you are man – always there for a brother.

JAMES

Thanks. I'll pay you back, promise.

CHESTER

When? I thought that Marigold chick was helping you get published.

JAMES

Yeah, but I won't get a check for two weeks.

Four Men in Paris

CHESTER
Crazy. You won't catch me working for magazines again – I can't work on other people's time.

JAMES
Well, we all can't be rolling in the dough like Mister Chester Himes. Making money off dime novels.

CHESTER
Give the people what they want, you get paid. What can I tell you? And I just got an advance on my next book – The Big Gold Dream.

JAMES
More adventures of Gravedigger Jones and Coffin Ed?

CHESTER
Those are my boys! And folks are buying it up. There's a brother in the states named Van Peebles who's gonna make The Real Cool Killers a movie.

JAMES
There's a brother making movies in America?

CHESTER
He's an independent movie maker. He asked permission to turn it into a film. Why not? Let's see what he can do with it. Listen – don't tell Richard about my advance, okay?

JAMES
Why?

CHESTER
I don't need to hear his mouth. All that sugar water crap.

Four Men in Paris

JAMES

See? He's giving you hell just like me! I know where he's coming from – we have a responsibility as writers to talk about black issues..

CHESTER

No, man – I don't have any responsibility but to myself. The cause, the cause, the cause. Always about the cause. I spent the last ten years of my life, in and out of prison, about the cause. I'm done, man. I'm in Paris, I'm making money, I'm living for myself..

JAMES

And Fatima.

CHESTER

No. For myself. Ladies come and go. She's got a taste for black men.. I'll let her get her taste. But I don't make the mistake of falling in love. No need to be held down. Plenty of pretty ladies to indulge in.

JAMES

I hear you.

CHESTER

Sure you do.

JAMES

Hey listen – Time Magazine is looking for a correspondent.

CHESTER

Oh, really?

JAMES

To cover what's happening in the south.

CHESTER

Oh, isn't that rich. They don't wanna send any white folks down there – let's get a naïve young black reporter down there. Are you seriously thinking about going back to America?

JAMES

Well it could be a good opportunity.

CHESTER

Jimmy, don't be a damn fool – between the White Citizens Council, the Klan and the racist cops down there, you're gonna find yourself at the bottom of a swamp. Man, they've been protesting Jim Crow back when I was a kid – they were marching in the '30s, writing articles about the atrocities, the lynchings, the oppressive laws – oh, sure the Times writes an article or two now. No one cares, James. You think anyone in Congress gives a damn? What's Ike doing about it? Nothing. No one in power cares, no one who can make a difference cares.

JAMES

What about Brown v Board?

CHESTER

Sure, the Supreme Court says segregation is unconstitutional. That was six years ago. And nothing has changed.

JAMES

But the young people are changing. The marches, the sit-ins, the protests. Something new is going on there. Like these kids at Atlanta University wrote a manifesto..

CHESTER

James, c'mon man, I don't need a lecture..

JAMES

Listen – it's called An Appeal for Human Rights. They're talking about solidarity with all the protesters. These groups are joining together and working with each other. King is uniting with Core and the SNCC. We haven't had that partnership before. I don't know, man. I'd hate to wake up an old man, knowing I could have been part of this movement but chose to stay here. We could be a part of history.

CHESTER

Don't give me no "we", James. I don't need the guilt trip – I've written articles about the struggle – I wrote for The Crisis – I wrote If He Hollers Let Him Go – I've been in jail for the struggle. So don't tell me about some young kids that think they can make a change. If you wanna go, James – go. But let's be real. You know why you're here. You're here because you want to be here. You were in the skillet and you chose to get out of the fire. This is paradise – for all of us. So keep reading those Times articles and sit in that comfortable café chair here in Paris and talk about the struggle. But spare me the bullshit.

JAMES

Damn, man – I wasn't trying to lecture you.

CHESTER

Besides, aren't you enjoying yourself at the Blue Lounge? That special café on the other side of town?

JAMES

Where?

CHESTER

Listen – everybody knows what's going on down there. Hell man, I don't care, I don't judge who you are. But you ain't gonna find any blue lounges in Mississippi. The Times won't tell you that. And I bet you didn't even tell the Times.

JAMES
But that's not the issue.

CHESTER
James, I'm trying to help you out. Stay where you're comfortable. (FATIMA is seen) Excuse me for a moment, James.

FATIMA
I was looking for you.

CHESTER
Here I am. I thought you were done with me.

FATIMA
Done? **(Looking at JAMES)** Am I interrupting anything?

CHESTER
No, not at all.

FATIMA
Why am I done with you? I'm not upset.

CHESTER
You were pretty upset when you walked off last night..

FATIMA
I'm just shy. I don't know, Chester. **(Holding CHESTER's hands)** Sometimes I scare myself..

JAMES
(Hurt by the closeness of FATIMA and CHESTER) I'll talk to you later.

Four Men in Paris

CHESTER
(Starts to walk to JAMES) Hey James, don't get me wrong..

JAMES
(Walks away) it's ok. We'll talk later. **(Exits)**

FATIMA
I didn't mean to interrupt.

CHESTER
It's ok. James is thinking of going back to the United States, and wants me to join him.

FATIMA
Oh, the States. So you're going back?

CHESTER
Doubtful. **(Walking with FATIMA, arm in arm)** So why do you scare yourself?

FATIMA
Well, sometimes, when I'm with you, I feel things and I just get nervous..

CHESTER
You've been with a man before, right?

FATIMA
Very little.

CHESTER
You've been in bed with a man before, right?

FATIMA
Very little.

CHESTER
Uh, well. I didn't know. I guess I'll have to take things slow.

FATIMA
I know you don't want to hear that. But I really like you, Chester. I love your writings and I love how you carry yourself. I think you're a real man. But I just…..

CHESTER
Just what?

FATIMA
I want things to be natural. To last. I don't want to dream about you and wake up and you're gone. Or you like another lady and leave me. You know, my mom don't let me date men. Very protective. So I don't know men very well. But I listen to your stories and I see you with the other men and hear you talk and it's fascinating. It's like I'm in another world. I just want whatever we have to last..

CHESTER
It can last, but it takes faith. You have to trust me and I have to trust you.

FATIMA
You know people are very quick, as if the moment will pass if you don't grab it quickly. That's dangerous, you have to know what you want before you get it. I like to take things slow. Like a well home cooked meal. You prepare it, you sweat to put it together, but you cherish the meal because you know what it took to make it. I don't know if I make sense.

CHESTER
Yes, that makes perfect sense.

Four Men in Paris

FATIMA
Maybe I'm too slow for you.

CHESTER
No. Not at all. But when a woman says no to a man, he thinks there's something wrong with him.

FATIMA
No..

CHESTER
I know how us black men can be..

FATIMA
No, that has nothing to do with it. I just don't want to rush. I envy so much how you are close to your men friends. I want to be that close to you. So we can talk just like you talk with them.

CHESTER
Well, we've had history. Back in America.

FATIMA
Yes, in America! So if you go, I want to go too.

CHESTER
I'm not going. Paris is just fine for me.

FATIMA
What's wrong with America?

CHESTER
(Turns away) It's hard for me to explain. Constant rejection. Constantly explaining you're not a threat. Constant harassment. Getting screwed with. I mean, you'd do very well in America. But a black man.. **(shaking his head)**

FATIMA

I hear America is wonderful. Where people are free to do what they please. "Purple mountains majesties .. across the.. " I forget how it goes. But I hear such amazing stories. Beaches, mountains, skyscrapers, so many places to shop, so many things to do, and so much music! The blues, rock and roll, and country! I dream about America all the time, about working in an office, with high heel shoes, clicking on the city pavement with so many people around me, with money in my purse – being independent and free! Can't it be that way?

CHESTER

It's not that easy..

FATIMA

But you're a writer. You have money, you make money, right? We can do it together, in America, can't we?

CHESTER

Well, **(weakening)** as long as you believe, and you don't mind struggling..

FATIMA

(wrapping her arms around CHESTER) We can do it. I believe. I believe in us. And I believe in you. (kiss) I'm not afraid anymore. I don't want to lose you. I want us to be together.

CHESTER

(Touched) This gristled black man – this is what you want?

FATIMA

If we take our time, and learn, understand each other.. I'll give you everything. Promise. **(kiss)** Chester, I want you to marry me.

Four Men in Paris

CHESTER

(Closes eyes) Fatima, for a woman who wants to take her time, aren't you rushing things?

FATIMA

It's a fiancée visa. It takes six months. We'll have time to learn, understand each other. And then we go to America. Across the sea to a whole new world!

CHESTER

(Considers JAMES' conversation) Yes...it is a whole new world. Exciting things are happening there.

FATIMA

Really?

CHESTER

Yes… yes there are. Yes.. **(to FATIMA)** Yes, I'll marry you.

FATIMA

I'll make you happy, Chester, I promise**.** **(Enthusiastically kisses him – then grabs his arm)** Oh, my God! Quick, let's go to my Mom's house to tell her the good news!

****

ACT TWO, Scene 4. Richard's home. Richard is preparing to go to Ghana. ELLEN is in the kitchen. JULIA is offstage.

OLLIE

Ain't it funny what motivates a man. Velvet wanted Chester to take her to America to escape the police and.. whatever she did. James suggested we were missing on the emerging American Civil Rights Movement, but Chester poo-poo'ed that. But Fatima? Must be something in those twinkling eyes of hers. Maybe Chester never envisioned a young Parisian beauty would see so much goodness in that hard core black man. I imagine Ellen saw the same thing in Richard, when they were together, back in the 40's. Back then, they were young and vibrant writers for a Communist party – using their words to battle American capitalism, imperialism and to uplift the working man! And they uplifted each other. And they were so much in love. But in paradise, things change..

RICHARD

(Busy packing) I'll be back in a week.

ELLEN

You have a number?

RICHARD

I'll call you.

ELLEN

Richard, there's 100,000 francs missing in our account..

RICHARD

(Sigh) That's for the ticket.

ELLEN
The ticket?

RICHARD
The airfare.

ELLEN
They didn't pay for your ticket?

RICHARD
No, they didn't. They'll reimburse me.

ELLEN
When?

RICHARD
When it's all over. I'm gonna get paid while I'm there.

ELLEN
How much?

RICHARD
Ellen, don't start with me. You've been on me all week.

ELLEN
I don't want to start an argument. I'm just asking.

RICHARD
They're gonna pay me.

ELLEN
What are they gonna pay you?

RICHARD
I don't know how much – I'll find out when I get there and I'll let you know.

ELLEN
No, I mean what denomination?

RICHARD
(Pauses) I guess the pound.

ELLEN
Richard, Ghana isn't on the British pound anymore.

RICHARD
Well…

ELLEN
..they have their own currency. The Cedi. I asked the bank, they never heard of it.

RICHARD
You talked about this at the bank? Who did you talk to?

ELLEN
I don't know – I think a manager at the bank..

RICHARD
Why?

ELLEN
Because however you're getting paid, we need to cash it! They have to accept it at the bank.

RICHARD
(Restrained) Ellen – I have this all figured out. Please. Let me deal with it.

ELLEN
Ok, so did you figure all this out? Who did you talk to?

RICHARD
I'm going. I've got a half hour to get to the airport.

ELLEN
Did you talk to Chester?

RICHARD
Why?

ELLEN
He called. He mentioned if the police talked to you?

RICHARD
The police? No. Why?

ELLEN
I don't know. They visited him this morning.

RICHARD
I'll deal with this when I get back.

ELLEN
What is "this" – what's going on?

RICHARD
Nothing. **(To ELLEN)** Ollie mentioned to me that the cops was harassing Chester. He's messing with this French girl who's in trouble. It has nothing to do with us.

ELLEN
Then why would he say the police would visit us?

RICHARD
Chester's paranoid. He thinks the cops are scoping all of us out.

Four Men in Paris

ELLEN

What? Who?

RICHARD

Us. The four foreign black men. It's nonsense.

ELLEN

(Sitting down) Richard, you have to think about your visa status. You have to be very careful about what you do.

RICHARD

Ellen, please. You think I'm running around, chasing skirts?

ELLEN

No, I'm talking about what you write. These articles – what's in your books..

RICHARD

Ellen, cops don't care about what I write..

ELLEN

But some of the French citizens do. And certain people in Washington do. You have to think about this, Richard. They can screw up your visa – the American embassy. They can tell the French to restrict or deny you entry. You're writing bad things – about American racism and their hypocrisy in foreign policy.. and in this paper, you're blasting the British..

RICHARD

Wait a minute. You have a problem with what I write? You didn't before.. you changing on me?

ELLEN

I just want you to listen..

RICHARD
How is this different from what we were writing back in New York? We were placing international pressure on the American system by shaming the United States into changing. That's what we both did and we both believed in that. My writings – my shaming British imperialism – is the reason I'm visiting a free Ghana today! Don't you understand that?

ELLEN
I know that..

RICHARD
Then what's the problem?

ELLEN
I want to go to England. I told you that already. I want to relocate. Or eventually move back to America. We can't stay here forever.

RICHARD
(Resumes packing) I have to get out of here.

ELLEN
If you piss them off, they'll revoke ALL OF OUR VISAS – even Julia's. Don't do that to her. Just be careful in what you say, when you speak in Ghana.

RICHARD
Go back to America?! Do you remember what we left – getting screwed by our wonderful communist friends on one end and the racist whities in the south on the other end? What about your parents who disowned you? Our commie comrades who threw me out of the organization when they asked me to STOP writing about blacks and write for their cause? Asking me to pick cotton for them? That's what you want me to go back to?

ELLEN

America's changed, Richard. Do you really want us to stay in Paris forever? I can't get a job here!

RICHARD

What I want is a woman who will be obedient and loyal to her husband. **(This hits ELLEN hard)** I don't know who you've been talking to, who's trying to manipulate you, but I sew seeds with my books. Seeds of revolution. I'm not stopping. No, I may not get paid, like our good friend Chester who's feeding sugar water to the masses. Or Jimmy who squeezes a paragraph or two out for French magazines. I write volumes! I write books. They're hard. They're rigid. They're stone. It's what you build revolutions with. Remember that. **(ELLEN just looks at him – RICHARD kisses her cheek)** Julia – kiss Daddy. **(JULIA runs and kisses daddy's cheek, then falls in ELLEN's lap)** I'll be back in a week. **(Struggles to find words)** I'll be back in Paris. Everything – will be fine.

ELLEN

(Stoic) Sure. **(With a forced smile)** Sure they will.

RICHARD exits, perhaps through the audience aisle, with his bags, while a lone light shines on ELLEN and JULIA. OLLIE is off SL, barely visible to the audience.

OLLIE

I had an old ex tell me: y'now, men are the last to know. I said, baby, what'chu talking about? And then she told me it was over. She was right – she knew a while back that it was over and I was the last to know. I guess we can delude ourselves. Fantasies can do that sometimes – delude you – and you know us writers. Always buried in our papers, writing away, creating our own worlds. Sometimes, not even paying attention to the world already around us. What's gonna happen to Richard? Will Ellen be there when he returns? What about Velvet? She gonna find

Four Men in Paris

out about Fatima and Chester? Will Chester join Jimmy in marching in Birmingham, Selma, Montgomery – or will he be tucked away, quaintly in some flat in Greenwich Village with Fatima by his side? And what about Jimmy – will he ever be free? Don't know 'bout you but I'm tuckered out! I need a break, don't you? Let's pick it back up in fifteen minutes. I'll see y'all!

END OF ACT TWO

INTERMISSION

Velvet and Chester

From left to right: Helaina Alvarez (Fatima), Barry Graves (Richard), S. Angelo Acevedo (Chester), Michael Dorado (Sartre), Pete Fitzsimmons (Ollie), Laura Michler (Marigold) and Curtis Manning (James)

Four Men in Paris

S. Angelo Acevedo as Chester and Helaina Alvarez as Fatima

Kim Donovan as Ellen and Barry Graves as Richard

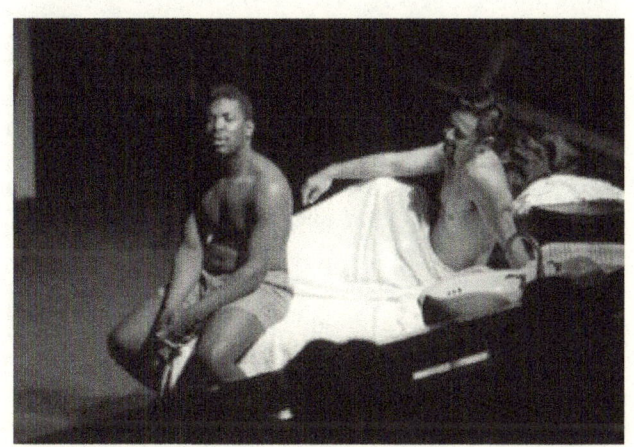

Curtis Manning as James and Joshua Flores as Francois

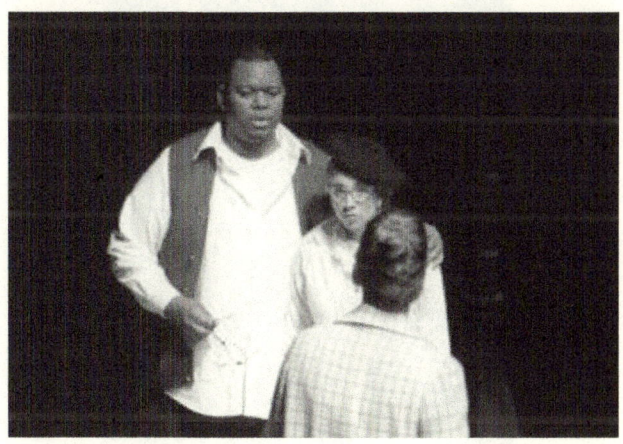

Barry Graves as Richard, Helaina Alvarez as Julia, and Kim Donovan as Ellen

Barry Graves as Richard, Reg Clay as Dr. King and Pete Fitzsimmons as Ollie

Barry Graves as Richard and Pete Fitzsimmons as Ollie

Four Men in Paris

Pete Fitzsimmons as Ollie

From left to right: S. Angelo Acevedo as Chester; Barry Graves as Richard; Pete Fitzsimmons as Ollie; and Curtis Manning as James

Four Men in Paris

FOUR MEN IN PARIS

ACT THREE, Scene 1 – Francois's room. Morning. JAMES and FRANCOIS are in bed. JAMES sits up and looks out the window, sitting on the edge of the bed.

FRANCOIS

How are you feeling?

JAMES

Hmm?

FRANCOIS

How are you feeling?

JAMES

I'm doing good. Relaxed.

FRANCOIS

You're in thought. What's on your mind.

JAMES

I received a telegram yesterday. Life Magazine. They have a job for me in America.

FRANCOIS

You didn't mention that last night.

JAMES

I know.

FRANCOIS

Will you take it? After what you had to go through in the US? You know things are still very bad there.

JAMES
You're right.

FRANCOIS
You're better off here.

JAMES
Right.

FRANCOIS
So... anything else on your mind?

JAMES
Just things.

FRANCOIS
(Embraces him from behind)
It's not good to hide things..

JAMES
I'm not. I certainly didn't expect this.

FRANCOIS
We had a nice time last night, didn't we? Isn't it what you wanted?

JAMES
Sure...

FRANCOIS
This doesn't have to be a fling. You can stay here. No more hotels. I make good money from the café and you with your magazine articles, we can combine our income, save some money and even buy a house in the villa.

JAMES
You've got it all planned out, I see.

FRANCOIS
I've got dream, James. I've always had them, but they've always been dormant. I just needed a little water to make them blossom. And here you are. *(kisses him).* I can't tell you how wonderful I feel. This is just what I needed. You're just what I needed.

JAMES
(Walks away from the bed, goes to sink to put water on his face)
Francois, we hardly know each other. Listen, last night was nice. Refreshing. But things are complicated..

FRANCOIS
Ok. Tell me. Explain to me.

JAMES
It's nothing. Just things I have to work out for myself.

FRANCOIS
You seem troubled..

JAMES
Francois, it isn't you..

FRANCOIS
I know it isn't me. I don't think it's you, either. You are carrying a cross, James. But who built the cross? The outside world? The "hetero's"? Those who want us to live by their rules? You have a right to be happy – to be who you are.

JAMES
Do you know who I am? This man you say you love, do you know me?

Four Men in Paris

FRANCOIS
James, you're gay. It's ok to say it.

JAMES
I'm a Christian. A boy raised by his mother and the church in Harlem, New York. A black writer that has a contract – a syndication – with several newspapers and magazines.

FRANCOIS
I don't understand, what does that..

JAMES
You think it's that easy? To walk out on the streets, holding your hand and telling the world, here we are? You and me, together? Men in love? Listen, we had a good time..

FRANCOIS
So you'll put on that three piece suit of yours, sit behind a typewriter and pretend to be Richard or your other friends? That's the answer? Pretend to be one of the boys?

JAMES
No, that's not it. And Richard has nothing to do with it.

FRANCOIS
Don't bullshit me, James. You're 36 years old, you're not a little boy anymore. Sure, you peep your head out of the closet and there's the father, peering down on you..

JAMES
That's not it! To hell with Richard! Don't you understand, I can lose my job! I can lose my syndication. Sure, folks in Paris don't care, but I'm still making money in America – I'm still writing for the black community – listen, there is an image they want and I have to provide it.

Four Men in Paris

FRANCOIS
What are you talking about? James, you wrote Giovanni's Room. People already know.

JAMES
(resigned, starts putting on his clothes and tries to leave) Let's not talk about that. I have to go.

FRANCOIS
Giovanni's room – James, it's a great book – the first of its kind. A modern telling of the gay experience. The passion, the love and the crucifixion of the homosexual. It's what the world needed to hear.

JAMES
(Stops, sits with Francois) I told the publisher to burn that book. (sighs) Yes, I wrote it. I opened up everything I had in it. I had a teacher in school tell me to be sure to distance yourself from your work – you can't work out your shit with your art. It can be therapeutic, but not therapy. You have an audience – focus on them, not you. I believe in that. But Giovanni's Room – I wrote about everything I felt, everything I had – I don't even know why I did or who would even read it. Or what it would do to me. You know, I still can't look at my family in their eyes anymore.

FRANCOIS
James, you wrote it because you had to! You had to show the world who you are – who WE are. We are Giovanni – we're wild, we're caged up, we want to live, and we want to love.

JAMES
I'm not Giovanni, Francios. I'm David. The man who destroyed a relationship.. succumbing to .. (looks at his hands).. desire.

FRANCOIS
Don't you dare say sin.

Four Men in Paris

JAMES
Fine, I won't say it. But it's all in there, isn't it. Giovanni – tortured and executed for love. Extreme passion that took him too far. David too.

FRANCOIS
So you're saying David should've just stayed at home, married Hella, have kids and that post-Puritan nuclear family life? You can't really believe that.

JAMES
I'm saying you can't always have everything you want. You accuse me of being a child, afraid of leaving the closet. A child is one that grabs everything it can and stuffs it in his mouth. No control. This is control. I have to control myself..

FRANCOIS
Bastard! Go away, James..

JAMES
Don't be upset, Francois..

FRANCOIS
Control? What about courage? The courage to look at all of them in the face and say – I'm gay! This is what I am and fuck you if you don't like it! That's courage – and there's nothing childish about it! But you don't have that courage, James. That's the tragedy. Your tragedy.

JAMES
You're only saying this because you want me to be with you. Just like Hella in the novel, you spit on me for not adhering to your dreams. It's ok, I'm used to it. The church spits on me for not being Godly. Richard spits on me for not being the proper son.. and now you, a man so beautiful, I never thought I'd dream to have my arms around. Someone so tender, pure and strong. And you care – I know you care for me. We wouldn't be arguing

like this if you didn't care. But this is my fault. I exposed my body to you but not my mind, not fully. So here it is. Francois, yes, I am a gay man. But I'm also a black man. And a child of God.

FRANCOIS

Listen to yourself! It's madness! You can't be all three – and James *(pointing to the window),* they will NEVER love you like I will. They will always despise you, always step on you, always pin you down with their rules. *(embraces him)* honey, I'm not spitting on you, I'm sorry if you think I am. James – stay. Do it for you. Do it for me. You can't look in your family's eyes, then look in mine! I can be your family. We can build a family. You said it yourself – Paris is paradise. Let's make it a real one. No more burdens. No more pain. If we live in secret, so you can still write your articles, then fine. Let's be together. James – Giovanni's Room was a dark room, where the windows were covered in shades. Step out of the room. Step in the light.

JAMES

(pulls out a letter, reads) "Mr. Baldwin – I hope this letter finds you healthy and well. As you may know, we are embarking on a series of Freedom Marches and we are looking for experienced writers to do correspondences for our magazine. We are looking for stories in Selma, Montgomery, Jackson Mississippi and other places in the south. We will pay generously per article. We believe history is in the making and we want only the best on the front line. We know you are in Paris and we have no problem clearing your visa, paying your airfare and setting up amenities while you're in America. Please write or call at your earliest convenience." *(holds up letter)* Time Magazine. Out of all of us – Richard, Ollie, Chester – they wrote to me.

FRANCOIS

You said you weren't going. We just talked about this. James – you can't. It's the south. You'll be killed.

JAMES

It's dangerous. I know. They'll cut me a check and throw me out in the wilderness. But as a friend once told me *(smiling to Francois)* – I need courage.

FRANCOIS

Don't do this, James. They can find someone else. Stay with me.

JAMES

(kisses him) I have to do this. But thank you for the memories, Francois. I'm sorry. *(Francois storms to the bathroom. James quietly leaves)*

****

ACT THREE, Scene 2. Main café. OLLIE and JAMES are there.

OLLIE

Everything ok, man?

JAMES

I'm ok.

OLLIE

You sure?

JAMES

The French magazine rejected three of my articles. They're not writing any more checks. I'm not getting paid. I can't even find Marigold anymore. She moved out last week.

OLLIE

I haven't heard a word from Chester. You hear from him?

JAMES

No, thought he was hooked up with that woman..

OLLIE

Which one? Maybe Fatima – he put in for a fiancée visa couple of months ago, but the way things are going, they may not give it to him. And that Velvet's been looking for him real bad.

JAMES

Really?

OLLIE

Oh yeah – he moved out, didn't tell her where he was, and she's been searching for him everywhere. That woman is crazy!

JAMES
(To himself) Richard…

OLLIE
What about Richard?

JAMES
Listen, I don't mean any ill will. Richard's been good to all of us. He was the first one here and hooked us up til we got ourselves situated. But that damn speech in Ghana – that really pissed off Washington!

OLLIE
You telling me! London too.

JAMES
All the good work the civil rights workers are doing in America and Richard has to spit on America like that? Why the hell did he have to mention Jim Crow and slavery? They're Africans! They don't know anything about that – that's not their history.

OLLIE
Dick was just making a connection between American brothers and the Africans

JAMES
I tried to call a publisher in Chicago and he hung up on me! Dick's poisoning all of us!

OLLIE
Come on, man.. he's in bad shape. Apparently he got some bug in Ghana – really messing with his blood.

JAMES
Well Ellen'll take care of him.

Four Men in Paris

OLLIE

Man, they've been in in some serious fights. And you know they took his passport..

JAMES

What??

OLLIE

He came back home to Paris. At the airport, he showed them his passport – and they took it. Man damn near got arrested, he was so upset. He called me to pick him up.

JAMES

They took his passport?? God damn! I put in a visa application to go back to New York

OLLIE

What? You're going back?

JAMES

You better think about leaving too. Or else we'll all be trapped here. Why do you think I can't get work here anymore? Why are the cops checking us out all of a sudden? The US Embassy giving me absolute hell! Thinking we're all a part of what Richard's thinking! They damn near took my passport away!

OLLIE

But they didn't.

JAMES

No. **(Pats breast pocket)** I got it. And I'm not leaving it in the hotel room or anywhere else. It's the only way I got out of here. I'm going back, man. You should too.

OLLIE
I know, brother. I've been thinking about it.

JAMES
Well you better get a ticket now. And make sure your visa's straight. That's it – I gotta go. I gotta get out. Don't hesitate, Ollie. Get out while you can. **(Exits)**

****

ACT THREE, Scene 3. RICHARD and **ELLEN's** apartment. Early evening. **JULIA** is offstage, in her room. **RICHARD** is haggard, nagged by persistent stomach pains and a horrible cough, but still well dressed in a shirt (no tie) and slacks. **ELLEN** looks tired. They have been arguing for hours. There's a small liquor cabinet downstage right. Both have been drinking a bit.

OLLIE
There's something about a ticket in your hand. Most the time, it's good news! And I'm not talking about a traffic ticket. I mean a ticket to travel – either on vacation or to start a new home. When we each got our ticket to Paris, it was a wonderful moment, it meant something special to each of us. But if you really think about it, when we go away from somewhere – especially very far – usually, you're running away. What it is we're running away from? But I'll tell y'all something ya probably already know: some stuff you can't run away from. Some places in the mind – unresolved issues, past pains, haunted histories – some places they ain't got no ticket out of. Best to just deal with what's staring you right in your face..

ELLEN
I went to five banks today

RICHARD
Let me deal with it?

ELLEN
How? You haven't been out of the house in a week.

RICHARD
Right. I'm sick. And look how you're treating me?

Four Men in Paris

ELLEN
How I'm treating you? I'm taking care of you. But Richard, I can't cash the check! Nkrumah gave you a check we can't cash.

RICHARD
I'll talk to him or one of his people.

ELLEN
Didn't you call him yesterday?

RICHARD
I left a message. This is a new government. I'm sure they have things going on..

ELLEN
We don't have any money! We're out.

RICHARD
How? I thought we budgeted..

ELLEN
You said Paul was working on getting you an advance on Island of Hallucination. That was two months ago.

RICHARD
Wait – when did we run out of money?

ELLEN
We talked about this already. I told you months ago that we had to slow down.

RICHARD
What did you buy?

ELLEN

Stuff for the house. The usual. What I didn't do was bail James out of jail, give him an advance..

RICHARD

Wait – I didn't give Jimmy an advance..

ELLEN

And buy a round way ticket and hotel fees to a Ghana conference they *invited* you to!

RICHARD

I didn't give Jimmy –

ELLEN

Don't lie to me! Ollie told me.

RICHARD

What are you talking to Ollie for?

ELLEN

He called, wanted to check up on you. Why can't I talk to Ollie?

RICHARD

What did you tell him?

ELLEN

Richard – where are we going to get money from? Whatever's in the fridge, that's it. Until you get paid next. You understand? That's it. And we can't make Julia's school payment. You said you'd handle this. And you're not. We had a bargain. I'd take care of the house and Julia. You'd write the books and make the money. We haven't seen anything since The Long Dream.

RICHARD
Ellen, I know. For God's sake, what time is it?

ELLEN
And I know there's going to be a French play on the Long Dream.

RICHARD
Ellen, what time is it?

ELLEN
11:30. **(pause)** Did you give them money to produce the Long Dream?

RICHARD
I'm not talking about this.

ELLEN
I can't function like this..

RICHARD
You can't function like this?

ELLEN
You won't tell me anything.

RICHARD
You can't function like this? And what good is telling you anything? You'll just use it against me. **(Frantic)** Look, things are rough, but we'll get through. We always do. Listen, we have to hold on, to keep things together. Look, there's gotta be a bank that can cash the check – I'll go in, they'll listen to me. I'll call Paul again. Hell, I'll call Ed Aswell..

ELLEN
Ed?? After you dumped him for Paul? When is the last time you talked to Ed? Is he even alive still?

RICHARD
I'll find out.. I'll figure it out.

ELLEN
You haven't figured it out for a while now, Richard. And now you don't have a passport.

RICHARD
Ellen..

ELLEN
How are you gonna fix that? I warned you, didn't I? You went to Ghana and you shat all over the United States and you didn't think the American Embassy in Paris would get wind of it? And make a phone call to make sure your passport got revoked? You don't listen – I told you they would do this. I told you to be careful of what you say. And I told you about the Ghanian currency. They didn't even have the decency to give you money, they gave you a check! This is ridiculous! I can't do this..

RICHARD
(Embolden – he's had enough) Well you have a choice, Ellen. Your visa's still good. You have a passport. I told you a long time ago that I'm a political critic. And I'm suffering for my work – the type of suffering other artists wouldn't even dare to try to endure. So they fucked me over with the money. They're a young country, they're struggling, just like I am. Just like all of our brothers. What good is the black race if we lock ourselves up in our gated community once we made it, and let our brothers outside our gates suffer? What kind of a man would that make me? Aw, what's the point – how can you understand? **(beat)** it's hilarious, really – that I ever thought you COULD understand..

Four Men in Paris

ELLEN
Really? Is it hilarious? You enjoy seeing me suffer?

RICHARD
You're suffering?

ELLEN
I'm at home all day! I have to strategize whether to buy milk or sugar, or meat or vegetables – what to cut out, what to hold on to – telling Julia we're only eating a half plate this evening and sending her to be hungry – is that funny? Not knowing how to talk to people on the streets, not having any friends and not knowing what my husband's doing or how he's going to bring in the money – holding on to your dreams and giving up mine, trying to figure out what insanity you're writing and who you're going to piss off and how it's going to affect all of us.. you talk about the suffering – Richard, I think you ENJOY suffering. You enjoy talking about it. Always bringing up the past like it's a proud badge. It's old, Richard. No one wants to hear it anymore. That's why you're not selling books. Chester has a three bedroom flat and he's a single man! No wife, no kids, no worries. He's got the kind of income we need! But no, you won't "stoop that low". Richard, your wife is suffering. This isn't what I asked for. I know this is hard, but I'm trying to help you understand. Richard? Are you listening?

RICHARD
(a long pause) Suffering. Hm. Ellen?

ELLEN
Yes?

RICHARD
How long have you been black? **(Pause – Ellen doesn't answer)** Tell me. How long have you been black?

Four Men in Paris

ELLEN
(Softly, bluntly) I'm not black.

RICHARD
THANK YOU! Suffering? You've suffered? We have a half loaf of bread instead of a full loaf, that's suffering? We have a two room flat in Paris – oh my God, how horrible! That's suffering? You have to suffer through the street among French people who have your same skin tone and for what it's worth, they probably already assume in their minds that you're French, too! Because you can blend in! But no, that's still so horrible for you because **(as if talking to a child)** you wanna talk to people. You don't have friends. Aww, poor baby! **(serious).** You ever get grabbed from the collar and have a southerner kick you out of a restaurant, with everyone looking, because of the color of your skin? You ever run like hell from a white mob because they accuse you of winking at a white girl? You ever have your momma, your uncle and all the relatives of your family empty out their life savings just to buy you a nice suit and a ticket to New York because you were the only one in the family – in three fucking generations – to go to college? And you've got mixed feelings of pride and guilt because you took their life savings and you wish they didn't have to live in an oppressive world where your family's only hope for survival is you? You ever feel that burden, Ellen? You ever carry that cross? You ever beg to white members of a book club, like a beggar with a cup in his hand, hoping they'll read your little book? Hoping those whities will give their blessings and transform you, with their magic wand, into a published writer? No, you never had to go through that, Ellen. You were friends with them – those were your pals – of course they publish your book. No I had to beg! I had to make adjustments in my writing to not piss off their sensitive white ears!

ELLEN
We're getting off track..

RICHARD

SHUT UP! Don't give me that shit about suffering – what the fuck could you know about it? What about the commies that welcomed me in and then threw my black ass out because I wouldn't write for them? Dealing with assholes like Jimmy and Langston who stab me in the back even when you push for their works to be published? Did you suffer, Ellen? Do you really suffer? Like Bigger Thomas?

ELLEN

Stop it!

RICHARD

You Bigger, Ellen? You ever escape a lynch mob, Ellen? Can you write about it – tell us all about the sufferings of your life? Were you ever called a dirty little nigger boy who ain't gonna be nothing and will never be nothing? Have you? Suffer – bitch, please! Shut the fuck up and get me a drink!

ELLEN

(**Furious**) You want a drink? You want a drink?

ELLEN goes to the liquor cabinet, grabs a bottle and throws it at RICHARD's head. RICHARD attacks ELLEN center stage, even knocking over the CS table. ELLEN grabs another bottle and starts beating RICHARD when JULIA intervenes, pulls ELLEN away SR while RICHARD cowers SL.

JULIA

Mommy! Stop!

RICHARD

Are you out of your mind?

ELLEN
God Damn You! God Damn You, Richard!

RICHARD
This is one hell of a relationship.

ELLEN
Is this what you wanted? Is this what you wanted? You want me to go back in the kitchen and fix you a sandwich, right? Well fuck you, Richard. I'm not doing this anymore.

RICHARD
No, what YOU want is to be the white master now. I'm not a subservient to anyone. You hear me? Not even you.

ELLEN
You're sick. How can you say that?

RICHARD
We might as well let the truth out now! I know that's what you wanted. I don't know who you've been talking to. Who poisoned you, Ellen. You can't stop me. You can't stop me from writing!

ELLEN
No one's trying to stop you, Richard.

RICHARD
You can't stop me.

ELLEN
You're not listening. You never did. **(to JULIA)** We're leaving. Get your things.

RICHARD

Leaving where?

ELLEN

I have to get out of here. There's a hotel on Boulevard St. Germaine..

RICHARD

Ellen, wait a minute.

ELLEN

No – I'm the bad guy, right? The white establishment, right? After everything I've done for you? Julia, get your suitcase and pack your things.

RICHARD

Ok.. I shouldn't ..

ELLEN

Don't even bother to apologize. How dare you say that to me. Tomorrow, I'm flying to England.

RICHARD

Ok.. I'm sorry. Stay. Ellen.

ELLEN

JULIA, LET'S GO!

RICHARD

You can't. You can't do this to me.

ELLEN

I have a passport. You don't. You can't stop me.

JULIA

I don't want to go.

ELLEN

What?

JULIA

Daddy needs us. He's sick.

ELLEN

Julia, you're coming with me.

JULIA

I don't want to go!

RICHARD

At least, let her finish her school year here.

ELLEN

(stewing – at RICHARD) Daddy's little girl, eh? **(beat. To JULIA)** Fine. You take care of your father. I'm going to buy you a ticket, too. You can use it anytime. When you get tired, call me. **(hugs JULIA)** Mommy will always love you.

ELLEN quickly grabs luggage and exits. Lights stay on RICHARD, siting, and JULIA behind him, resting her hands on his shoulders.

RICHARD

She'll be back..

Four Men in Paris

****

ACT THREE, Scene 4. On the streets. Late at night.

OLLIE
I wonder if Richard even knew Ellen had that much anger in her? You see, Dick had a way of pushing people's buttons – Chester's used to that back and forth, given his background and that he's known Dick for so many years. They're like brothers. James was too sensitive. Me, I'm just a cartoon artist, Dick don't screw with me. But man, you gotta be careful with how you talk to your women. My mamma always says you always hurt the ones you love. Ain't it a shame when you gotta run away FROM your dreams? But here's a man who's running towards his dreams..

CHESTER
It's all set now

OLLIE
So you're serious!

CHESTER
Yeah, man. Fatima's it – she's the one. And I got the F-1visa done and I got tickets in my pocket!

OLLIE
The finacee visa?

CHESTER
Yeah – but man it's tough at the Embassy. They're still pissed at Richard, but I told them – hey, I do dime novels, I don't mess with the political crap. Hey – one dude there's a fan of mine! He had a copy of my book and I signed it for him.

OLLIE
Look at you, big shot!

CHESTER
Helps, man. But it ain't helping me with the rollers.

OLLIE
The cops?

CHESTER
They've been at my house every other day! They swear Velvet's with me and I'm hiding her – I haven't messed with that chick in a month!

OLLIE
And you know she's looking for you too.

CHESTER
Nothing like a woman to screw your game up. And I still haven't figured out what she did. I talked to one dude at a bar and he says she had some older husband and there was some insurance money involved. Dude died, but the autopsy at the time said was a heart attack.

OLLIE
Well, he was an old man. His time to go, right?

CHESTER
She could have murdered him. Get that insurance money or clean out his account. She's about her money, all right..

OLLIE
Man, this sounds like it's right out of your book!

CHESTER
I write about drama, I'm not trying to have any, for real! After next week, I won't have to worry about it. It'll be just Fatima and me, going home to America.

OLLIE
I thought you frowned on good ol' Uncle Sam..

CHESTER
Well Jimmy talked to me about the movement going on over there. Some exciting things happening down south. A real coalition. He's right. They need writers. Someone to write the history. Who better than us, right?

OLLIE
I guess so.

CHESTER
So you're coming back, too? Better get that ticket now, man.

OLLIE
I'm worried about Dick. Did you hear the latest.

CHESTER
I heard his woman left him.

OLLIE
Man, hellova fight. A real mess.

CHESTER
That's on Dick. Screwing with us is one thing but not your wife.

OLLIE
Yup. **(in the shadows is VELVET, eavesdropping)**

CHESTER
Ellen's a solid woman – was there with him when the commies were screwing with him, when he was fighting to get some of his more controversial stuff published – hell, if it weren't for her, Dick wouldn't even be here in Paris! And taking care of Julia – you can't find a woman like that anywhere..

Four Men in Paris

OLLIE
Is this coming from master playboy himself? Is this the real Chester Himes?

CHESTER
Good looking women are a dime a dozen. Hell, in the right light, and some good makeup, some of the ugliest women'll look good to you. But a woman that's beautiful in the inside? Someone who sees in you all of her dreams and really uplifts a brother? Someone who sees in you something she wants to build a foundation on? That's the real thing. Ollie – I never told anyone this – but I never had a woman believe in me before. Even my momma thought I was destined to be a jailbird or a junkie on the streets. A good for nothing nobody. Even when you put on your best suit, looking good and you got money, some women will only see what they can get out of you.

OLLIE
Well, men do it too, partner.

CHESTER
Yeah that's true. So you play these games. Flirt, have a little fun and then it's over. But what happens when you take off that suit, put away the money and expose yourself – warts and all – and she still sees goodness in you? Isn't that what we've always wanted, as black men? Not to be seen as "negroes", but as real people. Who feel. Who think. Who dreams. Who wants the best in life and can offer the best in life. A complete man. Fatima really sees me, Ollie. This woman wants to settle down and have kids and she don't give a shit who looks at her cross-eyed because I'm black. That means something to me. Sure, it may be talk, but it feels different. She's willing to take a chance. To give it all for me. And I'm gonna give it all for her.

OLLIE

So no more women on the side?

CHESTER

Nope.

OLLIE

No more hanging out? Late night drinking?

CHESTER

Nope. I'm done.

OLLIE

You're gonna get that itch, partner. I know you.

CHESTER

No, man. She's it. And I'm the one for her. We're gonna take our time. A nice, slow, buttermilk bread in the oven home made love. And take a look at this – **(reveals a diamond ring, still in the case)**

OLLIE

Good lord! What is that, a 27 carat diamond? Man, that must have been half your advance!

CHESTER

Some things some things you can't put a price on, my man. Gonna give it to her tomorrow. **(pockets the ring)**

OLLIE

Hahaha – well, I'm happy for you man. So where is she now?

CHESTER

She's at home. Meet me tomorrow, we're gonna hang out at the café.

Four Men in Paris

OLLIE
Hey man – I'm bringing Dr. King next week to meet Dick. Join us.

CHESTER
King's coming?

OLLIE
Short visit. You gotta meet this brother. He's the face of the new black struggle.

CHESTER
All right! Lemme run and I'll hook up with you later. **(Exits)**

OLLIE
Now everyone thought Dick was at least ten years older than everyone else – cause of his demeanor, his lordly ways. What folk didn't know was that Chester was only two years younger – always athletic and graceful in how he moved. But this time around, he had a real bounce in his step. Like he could fly over the Eiffel Tower himself. Love is a wonderful thing when you feel that way..

(VELVET emerges from the shadows, ponders a bit, then takes out a pen and paper, sits at a café table and starts writing)

..but of course there's that other flip of the coin, when the one you love don't love you back. Oh, there's plenty of songs about it, right? **(looks at VELVET)** Course there's some folks that you aught not piss off. Dangerous folk. Velvet had to be quick – before Chester put that ring on Fatima's finger. Velvet had a plan. As old as that English bard way back. **(VELVET rips a sheet of paper she had written and holds it out – OLLIE takes the paper and reads. As he's reading, FATIMA appears SL – she's at home- and as OLLIE reads, he slowly walks to her,**

Four Men in Paris

and hands her the paper. In the end of the monologue, FATIMA grimaces and runs off stage. Also at the end, VELVET finishes writing and slams the pen into the café table, "impaling" it)

OLLIE
(as VELVET writes)

"Fatima, I wanted to write this letter and get it to you as quickly as I can. We've shared so many moments in our brief time together. And I know you're excited about our engagement and our future in America. But I have to tell you – it's over. I found another woman – very hot and very sexy – and we're leaving for America very soon. The fact is – I just don't love you. And I'm leaving without you. Honestly, you are boring, stupid and ugly. And you're lousy in bed. You just can't satisfy a black man like me. Let's face it, you're really just a little child and when you do a little growing up, then maybe I'll reconsider. In the meantime, say hi to your mommy and have fun in your little fantasy world. Don't bother writing back, I won't respond. Sincerely, Chester"

Before OLLIE speaks, lights go up to Richard's area – which is a mess.

Four Men in Paris

****

ACT FOUR, Scene 1 - CHESTER's apartment. VELVET is lying on his bed, prominently center stage, as before.

OLLIE

Now, the Paris Magistrate drew up an arrest warrant on one Chester Himes for harboring a fugitive. And for murder. Fatima read that letter, that spiteful, hated letter Velvet wrote – that was it for that poor thing. She took a bath and slit her wrists. Lord, her momma went nuts! Called the police, they found the letter, and the police went searching all over Paris for Mr. Chester Himes

CHESTER

(Barges in from imaginary SL door, and is shocked to see VELVET in his bed) Well, well. I'm not surprised. You found me.

VELVET

Miss me?

CHESTER

How did you get in?

VELVET

I have ways. **(Smiles)** The best things in life are surprises, Chester. Come, give me a hug. We're together again.

CHESTER

There's no we, Velvet. You've got cops have been all over my ass – ever since I met you. (beat) I know what you did.

VELVET

Me? You hearing rumors of me again? And pray tell what have I done this time?

Four Men in Paris

CHESTER
Fatima – the letter.

VELVET
Oh, the letter. Aw, she's hurt, no? Well, Chester, you shouldn't say such mean things to hurt her little heart. Now you won't be able to touch those knees..

CHESTER
You think this is funny? You like being this cruel, don't you?

VELVET
It took me weeks to find where you lived! Your friends wouldn't tell me, you stopped going to the café, you moved out of your last place. But I'm persistent. And when I want something, I find it. Remember what I told you- we're carnal. Like animals. We will get what we want.

CHESTER
Yeah, you found me. Let's give you a nice round of applause..

VELVET
Don't mock me, Chester. If she wants you so bad, then she'll come to get you. She'll forget that letter and come to you. Find you like I did. Let her put the effort like I do.

CHESTER
Come to me?? She's dead! She killed herself.

VELVET
What?

CHESTER
She killed herself in the bathroom – her mother found her with her wrists slit. You didn't know that?

Four Men in Paris

VELVET

(After a beat, erupts into uncontrollable laughter) You're kidding! She killed herself? She's dead? What a stupid girl. Over a letter? That's hilarious!

CHESTER

(Astounded) You have a lot of nerve.

VELVET

Wait – you blame me? How can you blame me? I write a letter – I was mad, I wanted to get back to her, she steal my man, so I get back at her. But I don't kill her. She kill herself. She's too dumb to find another man and end her life, why's that my fault?

CHESTER

Stupid little girl? That stupid little girl BELIEVED IN ME!! She told her family about me! That little girl had a dream, just like a fairy take Cinderella dream – of living in a world of peace and love and happiness – a new world where she can be whoever she wanted to be – and love that perfect man in her life. Her prince charming. And that was me, Velvet. I was her prince charming. And now she's dead. Y'now, I guess it's not your fault. It's mine. I came in her world and you came in her world – through me. You killed her through me.

VELVET

I got dreams too, Chester! But I'm a grown woman, not a little girl with stupid Cinderella dreams! I don't need no god damn prince charming. I want a real man – to walk with me, run with me, live with me, die with me and suffer with me. You know whats wrong with little girls like Fatima? She wilts under the slightest pain. A little letter and she dies. You think a fucking letter will kill me? Ha! I don't need to tell you how many men abuse me and try to kill me – I don't need to tell you about being raped and thrown away like a rag! Did I steal? Damn right I did – I had to survive! Did I lie to police? Yes, I lie. Because I know how to stay on top. I don't understand you – falling for her. She's a little doll. I'm a woman, Chester. You want a girl or a woman? Can you handle a woman, Chester? I'm a survivor, just like you, Chester. Can you handle me? Huh?

CHESTER

You're a survivor, all right.

VELVET

(Changes beat, softly) You can handle me, baby. C'mon – let's not fight. You have bags packed. I don't need bags. Take me with you, Chester.

CHESTER

You need a visa.

VELVET

You still have the fiancée visa? Under Fatima's name? Well... I can be Fatima for a day.. Ches-TER **(Giggles)**

CHESTER

You got it all worked out, don't you?

VELVET

Of course.

CHESTER

Did you have it all worked out with Michel?

VELVET

What?

CHESTER

You know, your elderly husband you poisoned a year ago? **(Silence)** I had a nice long conversation with the constable – the same one knocking on my door every other day looking for you.

Four Men in Paris   115

First autopsy said it was a heart attack. But the insurance agency did another autopsy – even after paying you the money. Arsenic. You killed him.

VELVET
No. That's a lie.

CHESTER
(Softly) Shame if they were. It's actually a novel idea. Something right out of my book. Hey, you said it already – we're both survivors. Me from the streets of Brooklyn, you in the streets of Paris. He was an old man, anyway. Who cares? **(she smiles)** Just promise you won't off me the same way you off'ed him.

VELVET
Never, baby. He's an old man. He use me, so I use him**. (both kiss)** When we're in America, they won't be able to touch us.

CHESTER
Very true. **(Walks over to the door, gestures to VELVET to follow him – VELVET dances to him. CHESTER opens the door where three OFFICERS come to arrest VELVET).** You get what you need?

OFFICER
Yes. Merci, Mister Himes.

VELVET
CHESTER!! WHY?

CHESTER
You know why. **(Police escort VELVET out – OFFICER talks to CHESTER)** You have a warrant for me too, right?

OFFICER

Well, you've been helpful. I do have a warrant. Who says it needs to be executed? Besides, you were never here.. **(Exits)**

CHESTER

That's right. I was never here.

CHESTER looks around his swank Paris apartment, picks up his bags and leaves.

****

ACT FOUR, Scene 2. RICHARD's apartment. Transformed from the last scene, it is dingy and dirty. Stacked dishes on the table and paper scattered on the floor. RICHARD is in his bathrobe, his disease is in its advanced stages. JULIA is offstage, but when she emerges, she's the same chipper, well kempt little girl from the earlier scenes.

OLLIE

Y'now some people we meet in life can catch us by surprise. You wouldn't even know how to act if they showed up right in your face! What would you say, how would you act. But I guess that all depends on who they are and what they mean to you. Well, today, Richard's going to meet a man who is a symbol of freedom to many men.. something Dick would have wanted to be.

RICHARD

(On the phone) Paul, please! All I need is a little something. Send something on the wire. Paul, listen to me. I don't have anything now. Ellen's gone, I don't know how much money she took.. what? You talked to her? When? What did she say? … no, no, she didn't leave me with anything. She's lying. .. Paul.. ok, ok, I'm not doing this back and forth – whatever she told you, you either believe it or not. You knew me a hellova lot longer than you knew her. Listen. Listen. Did you get my latest draft? I reworked Island.. I mailed it off a week ago. **(calling offstage)** Julia! **(to the phone)** Julia took it to the post office – **(to JULIA)** right, sweetie? You put it in the mailbox?

JULIA

Yup, just like you said. **(JULIA starts clearing off the table, putting dishes in the kitchen)**

Four Men in Paris

RICHARD
Check your mail again. I made some tweaks – they'll love it this time.. well ask them. What… wait, Paul, that's what I'm paying you to do.. well you know what I mean, when it gets published, then you get paid. Listen. Don't tell me that – what do you mean it's indecipherable? It's an existentialist look in the black mind. Paul **(stomach pains)** – listen, you're my publisher, why the hell am I trying to sell the virtues of my own writing to my own publisher? You're supposed to be selling it to them! Market it! What do you mean you don't have anything to work with? Paul… who? I don't care who else you have to see, you work for me! No, stay on the phone. Wait! How much can you send? **(Sigh)** Ok. Yeah, yeah, thanks. **(Hangs up the phone).** God damned that guy. **(Muttering to himself)** Shit. **(Walks to a bowl, inspects Francs – his last savings).**

JULIA
Dad. You know Ollie's coming.

RICHARD
(Disoriented) Yeah. Today? When?

JULIA
Right about now. The house is a mess. Help me clean it up?

RICHARD
It's only Ollie. I'm not worried about it.

JULIA
He says he's bringing someone.

RICHARD
Sweetie, you're stepping on Daddy's work – watch yourself! **(Kneels to the pile of paper)** Everything has to be in order. Now this pile is the rewrites of Island of Hallucinations, and this pile is.. uh.. yes, White Man Listen. Hah, that was a good one.

So this pile is archives. Right. And this one.. oh, that's Island too.. no, that's the play.. the play version. And then .. right, the Long Dream.. **(Breaking down)** .. no, gotta put things in order.. Island goes here – no, that's the manuscript. I mean the rewrites.. and the play goes.. no, that's White Man Listen. Gotta put things in order.. gotta.. things.. put .. things in order. **(Buries his head in tears – JULIA comforts him)**

JULIA
I'll take care of it, Dad. Don't worry about it.

RICHARD
(Collects himself) Sweetheart, I love you very much. **(Beat)** I have to send you to England. To be with your mom. You can't live like this..

JULIA
What about you?

RICHARD
I'll be ok. **(Brightly)** I'll be joining you guys later. Just after I finish some business.

JULIA
You're coming too? But your passport –

RICHARD
It's all straightened out. Good ol' Ollie took care of things for me.

JULIA
See? Mommy thought your friends were no good.

RICHARD
It's good to have friends. It's good to have family too. So **(Buzz of the door)** – so while I'm with company, I want you to pack up

Four Men in Paris

and get ready. Mommy left you a ticket. You're going to use it tonight. Ok? **(Buzz)**

JULIA

Ok, Daddy. **(To the door)** Coming..

RICHARD

Hold it. **(JULIA freezes and waits while RICHARD collects himself and through the body alone, transforms himself to his old, majestic self).** Ok. Let them in.

JULIA opens the door and in comes OLLIE and DR. KING (the actor playing CHESTER can double as DR. KING – DR. KING will always have his back to the audience – no one sees his face)

OLLIE

(Reacts to the squalid house, but quickly collects himself) Well, Richard, this is the man the whole world's been talking about..

RICHARD

Well, well.. Dr. King himself. What a pleasure.

DR. KING

The pleasure is mine, Mr. Wright. To meet the great man who wrote the great novel.

RICHARD

It's only a story. You're creating stories in the flesh. You're doing the real work. This is my daughter, Julia.

JULIA

(Curtsey) Hello, Dr. King.

Four Men in Paris

OLLIE
Richard, hope we're not disturbing you..

RICHARD
No, no, just organizing some papers.. uh.. it only shows the hard work – if it ain't messy, you ain't working, right?

DR. KING
Exactly. You should see my work area.

OLLIE
And he's got four kids at that. So you know how messy that home's gotta be..

DR. KING
Well, Coretta keeps a tidy house..

RICHARD
I'm sure she does. Take your coat?

DR. KING
I'm sorry, Mr. Wright, but I can only stay for a few moments **(RICHARD has a violent coughing spell)** Richard, are you ok?

RICHARD
A minor bug.

OLLIE
You taking your medicine, Dick?

RICHARD
(Ruefully) Yes. All of them.

DR. KING
Well, I'll be praying for you. I have a meeting in London. I'm giving a speech for some dignitaries.

Four Men in Paris

RICHARD
Beautiful. Keep preaching the word, Doctor.

DR. KING
Well, I'm only picking up that baton you've been running with, Richard. I know your service, your struggles. Our generation haven't forgotten what your generation has given to us.

RICHARD
Well, we've done our best.

DR. KING
And now, it's our turn. **(Checking his watch)**

OLLIE
I'll drive you back?

RICHARD
One thing, Doctor, if you don't mind. Julia! **(JULIA comes from her room. RICHARD to DR. KING)** Doctor, you have a wound in your chest. The book signing incident?

DR. KING
Of course.

RICHARD
Show that wound to my daughter, if you don't mind.. **(OLLIE protests, but RICHARD hold up his hand)** I want her to see the wounds of the struggle.

After a beat, DR. KING hands his hat to OLLIE and exposes his chest to JULIA (his back is to the audience).

RICHARD
This, Julia, is what happens when a black man fights for freedom in America. Thank you, Doctor.

DR. KING
(As he buttons himself back up) S
He was deranged. I'm praying for her too.

OLLIE
We better get going.

RICHARD
Ollie, can I speak to you for a moment?

DR. KING
I'll wait outside in the hallway**.. (exits)**

RICHARD
Julia, you packed?

JULIA
I think so. I'm leaving now?

OLLIE
What's going on?

RICHARD
You're taking Dr. King to the airport?

OLLIE
Yeah – his London flight.

RICHARD
(his voice breaking) Take Julia. She's got a ticket – see if they'll upgrade her flight.

JULIA
I'm leaving now?

RICHARD
Yes, sweetie. Get your things. Remember, I'll join you later. On a later flight. Just got to take care of some things here.

(JULIA goes to her room)

OLLIE
Richard – you don't have –

RICHARD
Sssshhhh – **(quietly)** take her. Ellen already knows she's coming. Just take her.

OLLIE and RICHARD give one long embrace. JULIA comes back with her suitcases. OLLIE takes them as JULIA hugs her father.

JULIA
Goodbye Daddy. I love you.

RICHARD waves as OLLIE and JULIA exit. If possible, a gush of wind blows the papers all over the room, engulfing RICHARD – this will happen as OLLIE starts his monologue.

OLLIE
Remember how I said that a man's the last to know? This time Richard knew. He knew his time was coming. He told the good doctor he had a mild bug. It was amoebic dysentery. Parasites terrorizing his stomach, sapping his strength, killing him slowly and surely, and none of the multitudes of pills the doctors gave to him helped at all. Some of us felt it pushed him further to the brink of death. Was there a conspiracy? Did the French lynch Richard Wright through pills and ambivalence to his pain? None of us know. But he knew he was going. And he couldn't let Julia see him go. And in the end, it was only him. Him alone. We all

Four Men in Paris

wanted to be there for him, to comfort him. But he wouldn't have it. It was just him and his writings. His novels. His haiku. His "children". His legacy..

The storm of papers die out, and Richard disappears.

And then that was it. He was gone. His written legacy is the only other thing left alive.

****

ACT FOUR, Scene 3. JAMES is on the street, his bags packed. FRANCOIS meets him.

OLLIE
Saying goodbye is always a hard thing. I remember when I left to fight overseas. Momma hugged me hard and filled my bags with biscuits and jam. Daddy was stoic. He stuck out his hand, we shook, and he turned away. Cold, like a rock. I loved him anyway. That was my dad. And that was his lesson to me. Say your goodbyes quick. Turn around. And get on to your business. That's the day I became a man.

FRANCOIS
James?

JAMES
You're here. Didn't expect to see you.

FRANCOIS
You were going to leave without saying goodbye?

JAMES
I'm horrible at goodbyes. I thought we did. I'm sorry.

FRANCOIS
I could never understand Americans – so glib, so chatty, yet so distant when it comes to matters of the heart.

JAMES
Manly pride, I guess..

FRANCOIS
Is that what it is? Straight men, I understand, but us..

Four Men in Paris

JAMES
Are we really going to discuss this again?

FRANCOIS
We don't have to. **(pause)** I heard on the news about Richard.

JAMES
Yes. Horrible. The details are still sketchy on what happened.

FRANCOIS
I heard he got a bug in Africa. You think there are other things going on? CIA? Poison?

JAMES
Too many rumors. Who knows.

FRANCOIS
What do you think?

JAMES
Whatever happened has happened. I can't focus on how he died. I do know how he lived. A little boy in Nanchez, Mississippi. He became the pride of Black America, a true legend.

FRANCOIS
There you go again. I don't understand you. How can you respect him when he never respected you?

JAMES
Of course he did. He got me jobs, he respected my writings – most of it anyway. He was my mentor. I had to learn from him. **(turns to audience)** You embrace your mentors and then you let them go.

Four Men in Paris

FRANCOIS
You've forgotten how he made you sulk at a bar after that party? And that's the man you want to lift up?

JAMES
Have you ever wondered why Jim Crow lasted so long? Not enough people spoke about it and those who did chose to turn their backs. Richard put a finger on what racism does to the black man – and woman. To our bodies, to our souls. He had his turn. Now it's my turn. People are marching. People are sitting in counters reserved for whites. People are being beaten. People are bleeding – shedding blood so a future generation won't have to. We won't be Bigger Thomas anymore. We won't be transformed as a result of hatred. We'll stand up and fight with dignity. It's a great story and it needs to be told. That's why I'm going. Do you understand now?

FRANCOIS
Sacrificing your true self for a group of people who won't embrace you for who you are? No, I don't understand.

JAMES
One day you will. One day, they will too. Especially if I give a part of myself to them. But they can't see me if I'm not there. That's the first step of loving someone, isn't it? Being there.

FRANCOIS
But you won't be here with me.

JAMES
(hugs him) There is a heaven that resides on the other side of hell. I have to make that journey to get there. But I will remember you. And our tender moment.

                             FRANCOIS
I hope they will love you, James. As I do. One last kiss? To remember you by?

(JAMES and FRANCOIS kiss passionately)

                             FRANCOIS
Au Revoir, James. Remember me. Take care of yourself.

****

ACT FOUR, Scene 4. OLLIE is center stage

OLLIE

What happens to a dream deferred? Does it dry up like a raisin in the sun? Or fester like a sore, and then run? Does it stink like rotten meat, or crust and sugar over like a surupy sweet? Maybe it just sags like a heavy load. Or does it explode? Hah, Langston could sure write. That's his poem. And we could all identify with it. Paris was like that beautiful sunrise in the morning, but sure enough, the sun faded and the sky grew dark. And before you know it, we were all gone.

But not all of us went back to America. I found my way to Deuschland, believe it or not! Yup, West Germany. Found me some solid work with two magazines and lived me a nice comfortable life.

(JAMES appears, SR) James did make it back – out of all of us, he was the only one who truly believed in the American movement. He had wanted to be the main writer of the movement and that scrawny little writer of essays – the least prolific of us all – became the greatest literary beacon of the Civil Right's Movement. His essay, Down at the Cross, documenting all the events: the march at Edmund Pettus Bridge, the bombing of those four little girls, even the great March on Washington – it put him on the front cover of Time Magazine. James Baldwin. He was on the mountain top. And he earned it.

(CHESTER appears SL) Chester thought about heading back, but he had a minor heart attack and a young writer named Lesley caught his eye. Messin' with them French women again. But this time it stuck – they eventually moved to Spain where they really did live happily ever after.

Four Men in Paris

(OLLIE steps away from DSC to the left, to reveal RICHARD behind him) Richard would have been proud of him. He also would have been jealous too. But Richard was there, on that mountaintop – but everybody can't stay on that top forever. America's not perfect, now, but it's close – so close to paradise. But Dick never saw any of it. Not the March in Washington. Not the Civil Right's Act in '64. None of the younger generations who became elected officials, superstars who are billionaires, and even a US President. Richard Wright, through his books, was our Moses, at least of our generation, and the paradise we experience now was one denied to him.

(Slowly, the four men form a line – some pantomime of talking and joking amongst one another while OLLIE speaks) But we did have fun – one brief, bright moment, where we black men were free, free as could be. In Paris. The sun will never shine so bright as it was back then.. when it shined on our faces – on the faces of Four Men – in Paris.

THE END

Playwright Notes

The black man's identity, especially his identity in America, has been a most debated subject – from W.E.B DuBois and Booker T. Washington at the turn of the century, to Tai-Neshi Coates and Dr. Cornell West of today, the black man has wondered where do we fit in our society – how much do we protest, how much do we acquiesce and when will we find peace. From Jack Johnson to Colin Kaepernick, the black man's identity in America has always been a never ending battle – a personal, bitter battle. This play reflects that battle – Chester Himes, seeing his reflection through the eyes of young love; Richard fighting demons beyond his reach; and James, battling his inner self to discover his true place in Black History. These aren't just the stories of four men who died long ago. This is our history – there is a black man in your life, if not you, who are a reflection of these black men.

My special thanks, firstly, to Richard Talavera, who created Before The Dream, a play on Richard Wright derived from the works of biographers that we performed ten years ago – a play that inspired and motivated me. My good friend Norman Gee, who through the Oakland Public Theater, sponsored readings of Uncle Tom's Children, which also inspired me. Playwright Scott Munson has been a mentor to me and I must give special thanks to his support and encouragement. Special thanks to the wonderful Karin and Jon Richey, the producers of Plethos Productions, that took a chance on a budding playwright – I can't thank you enough. Also to Gary Graves, artistic director at Central Works and teacher at the Berkeley Rep – the skills I learned from his playwriting course I will hold on to forever. Also to the wonderful folks at the PlayCafe for hosting the 2nd reading of Four Men, which helped in publicity and recruiting actors. And finally, my mom Rev. Joy Poindexter **Newman and my dad Reg Clay Sr. for always supporting me.**

Made in the USA
Las Vegas, NV
13 July 2023